AQA GCSE

ENGLISH AND ENGLISH LANGUAGE

REVISION WORKBOOK
Higher

Esther Menon Consultant: **Peter Buckroyd**

D1340968

Part of Pearson

Heinemann is an imprint of Pearson Education Limited, Edinburgh Gate, Harlow, Essex, CM20 2JE.

www.pearsonschoolsandcolleges.co.uk

Heinemann is a registered trademark of Pearson Education Limited

Text © Pearson Education Limited 2011
Edited by Vicky Butt
Designed and Produced by Kamae Design, Oxford
Cover design by Wooden Ark Studios, Leeds
Picture research by Elena Wright
Cover photo/illustration © Alamy Images: David Hoare
Printed in Malaysia, CTP-KHL

First published 2011

15 14 13 12 11
10 9 8 7 6 5 4 3 2

British Library Cataloguing in Publication Data
A catalogue record for this book is available from the British Library

ISBN 978 0 435 02727 8

Acknowledgements

The author and publisher would like to thank the following individuals and organisations for permission to reproduce copyright material:

PP3–7 Drinkaware leaflet: 'Your Kids and Alcohol', created by the Drinkaware Charity. Reproduced with permission of Drinkaware. P13 Transcript of speech 'Children in Trouble Campaign' by Martin Narey, former Chief Executive of Barnardo's. Reproduced by permission of Barnardo's. PP16–17 Article 'Cyberbullying' speech by Vernon Coaker, produced by nationalarchives.co.uk. P24 Cadbury Buttons advert. Reproduced with permission of Cadbury PLC. P25 Extract from 'Spurs to eat baby food' by Antony Kastrinakis. Copyright © The Sun, 10 November 2010/nisyndication.com. Reproduced with permission of NI Syndication. PP26–27 Article 'Baby food giant hails hungry adult market' by Kate Connelly, from The Guardian, 19 March 2010. Copyright © The Guardian News & Media Ltd. 2010. Reproduced with permission. PP37–38 Extract from 'Five Hours of Sport a Week for Every Child' from the Department for Children, Schools and Families. Crown Copyright material is reproduced by the permission of the Controller of HMSO and Queen's Printer for Scotland. P48 Article 'Shark Tales in South Africa' by Kevin Rushby, from The Guardian, 27 February 2010. Copyright © The Guardian News & Media Ltd. 2010. Reproduced with permission. P57 Advert 'Hello Boys' by The Autism Trust. Reproduced with permission of The Autism Trust. P58 Press release from The Autism Trust. Reproduced with permission of The Autism Trust. P77 Witney Firewalkers Transcript of Witney Firewalking Event. Reproduced by permission of Phototechniques Ltd. P84 'Review: Caroline Cardus sees How To Look Good Naked…With a Difference' from www.disabilityarts.org PP 91 & 99: Jorvik Viking Centre leaflet. Reproduced by permission of Jorvik Viking Centre. P88 Extract from 'All Points North' by Simon Armitage (Viking, 1998). Copyright © Simon Armitage, 1998. Reproduced by permission of Penguin Books Ltd.

The author and publisher would like to thank the following individuals and organisations for permission to reproduce photographs:

P15 Alamy Images: Mark Phillips; P18 Alamy Images: Mark Phillips; P37 Getty Images: Alistair Berg; P49 Alamy Images: Stephen Frink Collection; P50 Alamy Images: Stephen Frink Collection; P70 Alamy Images: LOOK Die Bildagentur der Fotografen GmbH; P80 Phototechniques Ltd; P85 Phototechniques Ltd.

Every effort has been made to contact copyright holders of material reproduced in this book. Any omissions will be rectified in subsequent printings if notice is given to the publishers.

Websites
Pearson Education Limited is not responsible for the content of any external internet sites. It is essential for tutors to preview each website before using it in class so as to ensure that the URL is still accurate, relevant and appropriate. We suggest that tutors bookmark useful websites and consider enabling students to access them through the school/college intranet.

Contents

Introduction

This Student Workbook is designed to help you target your revision and improve your grade in AQA GCSE English and English Language.

Some students think that because English and English Language is a skills-based exam that they do not need to revise. This is a myth! You can target your revision to improve your chances of getting a good grade. You should revise for English and English Language as much as for any of your other subjects, particularly because entry for so many jobs or further courses of study is dependent on how you do in your English and Maths GCSEs.

To achieve your best standard in the examination you must familiarise yourself with past papers. Use these, together with information from your teacher, to identify:

▶ your strengths, weaknesses and target areas

▶ what kind of questions to expect in the exam and which carry the most marks

▶ how the examiner will be marking what you write.

How to improve your revision techniques

1 **Use the specialists.** The first thing to do is to make use of the valuable resource of your teachers. During the period before the exams they will be discussing various tips for maximising your success. You might want to jot down your own code or symbol for top tips that are relevant to you, to help you when you revisit your notes. You must ensure you are clear about your own target areas: what exactly do you need to improve to achieve your target grade?

2 **Get organised.** So many students, even the most academically confident, begin their revision at a disadvantage because their books, papers and materials are in a mess. You might want to think about getting a folder or two and investing in a few highlighter pens before spending half an hour sticking in loose sheets and organising your notes. There are a regular handful of students I have taught over the years who were not naturally brilliant at English, but meticulous organisation, listening and hard work meant that slowly and steadily they overtook some of their brighter peers and achieved the highest grades.

3 **Know the exam paper.** Check that you are familiar with what the exam papers look like, how many marks are awarded for each question and how much you will be expected to write in your answer booklet. Work out how much time you should be spending on each answer and try to stick with that when you are doing practice papers.

4 **Discipline yourself to use a clear revision space.** When you are ready to revise, find a quiet area away from any distractions and don't fool yourself that browsing the Internet or staring at a computer screen or book is effective revision. Remember to take regular breaks and pace yourself. It is difficult to maintain your concentration span for very long periods of time. Breaking your revision into manageable sessions is much more worthwhile.

5 **Use a revision checklist.** For example, use the Revision planner on page viii of this Workbook. This could be a starting point for you to find out exactly what you know already and to help you find any gaps in your knowledge. It should discipline you to look at all the areas you need to revise, rather than just concentrating on the ones you find easiest or most enjoyable.

6 **Revise actively.** The most effective way to revise is through active strategies; these involve writing and thinking, not just staring at a book or screen. This means that you practise the skills you have studied, take part in completing revision activities and compare your answers with sample answers to see where you can improve your performance. Remember to use a clock to time yourself and keep up the pressure, mirroring exam conditions.

7 **Read!** Use a little of your leisure time to read texts from a variety of media, for example a broadsheet and a tabloid newspaper and adverts in magazines. Absorb the main story and viewpoint of the articles. Notice some of the features that you will need to consider in the exam, such as the main and supporting points, presentational features, intended audience and language.

8 **Check your work.** Read what you have written so that you can 'hear it aloud' in your head. Check that it makes sense. This is most certainly the 'boring bit' and many students simply fail to be disciplined enough to do this in the exam. For many of you working at the borderline between two grades, this can mean the difference between one grade and the next.

9 **Know what your target looks like.** If you are aiming for an A then make sure you know what one looks like. The GradeStudio activities in this Workbook will help you to identify how to improve your own work to match your target grade.

Revision checklist

How confident do you feel about each of the areas that you need to revise for your exam? Fill in the revision checklist below.

▷ Tick green if you feel confident about this topic.

▷ Tick amber if you know some things, but revision will help improve your knowledge and skills to the best they can be.

▷ Tick red if you are not confident about two or more aspects of this topic.

Section	Revision lesson (60–90 minutes)	Where to find more information to improve my skills	Skills to raise my grade	R	A	G
Reading	**1H** Evaluating the effect on the reader	**2** Read and understand texts: purpose and audience	I can make inferences about the viewpoints conveyed in a text.			
			I can explain how the content of a text has been tailored to its audience and purpose.			
			I can identify what a text assumes and implies about its audience.			
			I can select relevant evidence to support my points.			
Reading	**2H** Using evidence to develop a response	**1** Read and understand texts: finding information	I can confidently read and understand unseen texts.			
			I can interpret information and identify the viewpoint(s) being conveyed in a text.			
			I can select relevant quotations to support my points.			
			I can comment on and interpret those quotations.			
Reading	**3H** Comparing and cross-referencing texts	**7** Collate and compare	I can compare two or more texts': • content • audience • purpose • language features • presentational and structural features.			
			I can select and cross-reference evidence to support my opinions on the above.			
			I can explain these comparisons with insight and perception.			

Section	Revision lesson (60–90 minutes)	Where to find more information to improve my skills	Skills to raise my grade	R	A	G
Writing	**4H** Organising your ideas for writing	**9** Organise information and ideas	I can plan a series of points.			
			I discipline myself **always** to make a plan before I write.			
			I can sequence my planned points in a logical order.			
			I can structure and paragraph my writing to reflect my plan.			
Writing	**5H** Using a range of vocabulary and sentence forms	**10** Use language and structure	I can consistently write in sentences that are complete and grammatically correct.			
			I understand the terms simple, complex, compound and minor sentences.			
			I can write in simple, complex, compound and minor sentences.			
			I can choose particular sentence types to achieve particular effects in my writing.			
			I can choose vocabulary to create particular effects in my writing.			
Writing	**6H** Using a variety of punctuation	**11** Use and adapt forms	I can use commas, full stops, question marks, ellipses and exclamation marks.			
			I can punctuate direct speech correctly.			
			I can use colons and semi colons.			
			I remember to use a variety of punctuation marks in my writing.			
Writing	**7H** Proofreading	**12** Use accurate punctuation	I can recognise when sentences are secure or insecure.			
			I can use a range of punctuation accurately.			
			I can use a range of vocabulary that is accurately spelt.			
			I always proofread my written work.			
Writing	**8H** Writing to communicate effectively	**12** Use a range of sentence structures	I can identify the text type, audience and purpose required of a Writing exam question.			
			I can write in a variety of forms and demonstrate their appropriate presentational, structural and language features.			
			I can identify an appropriate register (when to write formally and when to write informally).			

Revision planner

Your school may advise you on how to use a revision planner or even provide you with a schedule. Of course, you will need to plan your English revision within a sensible schedule of revision for your other subjects.

You might like to use the template below to map out the time you will spend on each subject. This will help you discipline yourself to cover **all** subjects; we all tend to focus on what we enjoy and avoid what we find difficult! You might find it helpful to alternate revision of a subject you like, with one you find less enjoyable. Remember to plan in some treats and relaxation as well.

	WEEK 1	WEEK 2	WEEK 3	WEEK 4	WEEK 5	WEEK 6	WEEK 7	WEEK 8	EXAM DATE
Reading:									
1H Evaluating the effect on the reader									
2H Using evidence to develop a response									
3H Comparing and cross-referencing texts									
Writing:									
4H Organising your ideas for writing									
5H Using a range of vocabulary and sentence forms									
6H Using a variety of punctuation									
7H Proofreading									
8H Writing to communicate effectively									

What your GCSE exam paper looks like

Centre number					Candidate number	
Surname						
Other names						
Candidate signature						

AQA

General Certificate of Secondary Education
Higher Tier

English/English Language

ENG 1H

H

Unit 1 Understanding and producing non-fiction texts

Time allowed
• 2 hours

Instructions
• Use black ink or black ball-point pen.
• Fill in the boxes at the top of this page.
• Answer **all** questions.
• You must answer the questions in the spaces provided. Do not write outside the box around each page or on blank pages.
• Do all rough work in this book. Cross through any work you do not want to be marked.
• You must refer to the insert provided.
• You must **not** use a dictionary.

Information
• The marks for questions are shown in brackets.
• The maximum mark for this paper is 80.
• There are 40 marks for Section A and 40 marks for Section B.
• You are reminded of the need for good English and clear presentation in your answers.
• You will be assessed on the quality of your reading in Section A.
• You will be assessed on the quality of your writing in Section B.

Advice
• You are advised to spend about one hour on Section A and one hour on Section B.

---

front cover will
ays remind you
long you have to
plete the whole
er (2 hours)

---

e sure you
wer ALL of
questions

---

ck your answers
efully before the end
he exam because
rks on each question
given for sentence
cture, punctuation
spelling

---

marks for Section
nd Section B are
al so you should
de your time equally
ween the two
tions (about 1 hour
each section)

Using the Workbook

This Student Workbook has been written to help you to revise the skills and knowledge that you have covered in your AQA GCSE English and English Language course.

The Workbook has been designed for you to revise *actively*. There is plenty of room for you to write answers to the activities and practice exam questions. Throughout, you are encouraged to highlight and annotate exam questions and texts as you will in the exam.

Red:
I am not confident

Amber:
I am semi-confident

Green:
I am confiden[t]

Every lesson will open with the **Skills to raise my grade** table. You need to decide how confident you are with each of the skills listed. You can record your confidence using a traffic light system. The lesson then goes over these skills and at the end of the lesson you review your confidence. Hopefully your knowledge of the skills will have improved.

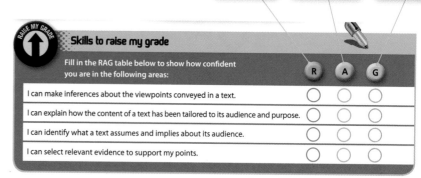

Skills to raise my grade

Fill in the RAG table below to show how confident you are in the following areas:

	R	A	G
I can make inferences about the viewpoints conveyed in a text.	○	○	○
I can explain how the content of a text has been tailored to its audience and purpose.	○	○	○
I can identify what a text assumes and implies about its audience.	○	○	○
I can select relevant evidence to support my points.	○	○	○

Each activity suggests how much time you should spend on it. This is for guidance only. Where you answer an exam-style question, the suggested timing will be linked to how much time you will have in the actual exam to answer this type of question.

10 minutes

Each lesson has a **Raise my grade** activity. In these activities you will practise the specific skills that you have revised in the lesson and try to improve a lower grade answer by one grade. This Workbook focuses on the Higher tier, so you will be looking at C–A* grades.

At the end of each lesson there is a **GradeStudio** section. This is to give you an opportunity to read examiner comments and grade criteria and match these to example student answers. This exam work should help you understand the grade criteria and how to maximise your grade.

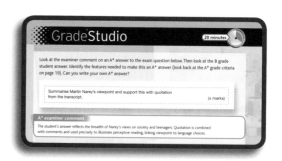

GradeStudio 20 minutes

Look at the examiner comment on an A* answer to the exam question below. Then look at the B grade student answer. Identify the features needed to make this an A* answer (look back at the A* grade criteria on page 19). Can you write your own A* answer?

Summarise Martin Narey's viewpoint and support this with quotation from the transcript. (x marks)

A* examiner comment

The student's answer reflects the breadth of Narey's views on society and teenagers. Quotation is combined with comments and used precisely to illustrate perceptive reading, linking viewpoint to language choices.

You can find answers to the activities online.

Good luck with your revision. As you begin the final countdown towards your exams, get ready to refine your skills and feel your confidence improve!

Personal notes and reminders

You may want to use this page to write down your personal revision targets, as well as any useful hints and tips you have learnt during your revision lessons to make your revision successful.

Skills you need ▶

You must show that you can:
- Identify the text type, audience(s) and purpose(s) of a text
- Establish how a text's content is linked to audience and purpose
- Understand what a text assumes and implies about that audience

The Higher exam will provide **three** texts for you to read and write about. You can't comment on the techniques used in a piece of writing unless you know **why** it was written (purpose) and **who** it was written for (audience). Before working on any of the texts you must therefore identify the **Text type**, its **Audience** and its **Purpose** (**TAP**).

The exam also requires you to read carefully. Any writer will have an intended audience and will predict what kind of views, knowledge and expectations that audience will have. You need to be aware of this in what you are reading.

This lesson will revise the process of anchoring a text by identifying text types, audience and purpose. It will support you in how to look out for evidence of what a writer is assuming and implying about his/her reader.

Add definitions for the following phrases:

▶ The 'TAP' of an unseen text means:

_____

▶ 'Implication' made in a text means:

_____

▶ 'Assumption' made by a text means:

_____

RAISE MY GRADE

Skills to raise my grade

Fill in the RAG table below to show how confident you are in the following areas:	R	A	G
I can make inferences about the viewpoints conveyed in a text.	○	○	○
I can explain how the content of a text has been tailored to its audience and purpose.	○	○	○
I can identify what a text assumes and implies about its audience.	○	○	○
I can select relevant evidence to support my points.	○	○	○

Activity 1

1 Write down the TAP of this text.

T: _____

A: _____

P: _____

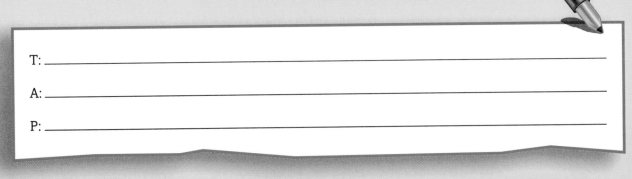

2 List the language and presentational features you would expect to find in the leaflet, e.g. bullet points, formal language.

Switch on the news or open the paper, and you're more than likely to see a story about **young people and alcohol**

Binge-drinking teens throwing up in the streets

Alcohol-fuelled crime and violence

Drink-driving accid

1

...It's enough to make any parent **panic**

The good news is there are fewer young people drinking, so a lot of the media coverage is 'hype'. However, those young people who do drink are drinking more. And let's face it: by the time they're in their early teens, most young people will have had an alcoholic drink.

That means it's crucial that young people have the most accurate information on the risks and issues surrounding drinking so they can make informed decisions. Parents are in the best position to give this information.

A recent Drinkaware YouGov poll showed over a third of 16 and 17 year-olds would prefer to get information on alcohol from their parents.

It's best to start early. Drinkaware research shows children's openness to their parents' influence changes dramatically as they grow up. Between the ages of eight and 12, children generally accept what their parents say about alcohol. From 13 onwards, young people increasingly pay attention to their friends. However, you may still have more leverage with your children than you might think.

If you're preparing to talk to your kids about alcohol, this leaflet will answer some of the questions you may have.

Growing numbers of children admitted to hospital with alcohol poisoning

2

3 Now look at the cover and the first two pages of the leaflet. Were your predictions about language and presentational features correct? Write down any additions or corrections below.

_____

_____

_____

20 minutes

Activity 2

1 Read the leaflet pages from Activity 1 in detail. List any assumptions or implications that are conveyed by the text and the images. Write them in the space below.

Assumptions that are conveyed by the text and images:

_____

_____

_____

Implications that are conveyed by the text and images:

_____

_____

_____

2 Explain how the presentational and structural features used by the writer link with the audience and purpose of the text.

_____

_____

_____

_____

Activity 3

10 minutes

If you want to simulate real exam conditions, keep to the 10-minute time allocation for this activity. If you want to practise structuring your answers and using point, evidence, explanation (PEE) as part of your revision work, you might want to spend longer.

Read the next two pages of the leaflet and then answer the exam-style question below. Remember to annotate/underline the text before writing up your answer.

How are presentational and structural features used on these pages? (8 marks)

How much is **too much** for under-18s to drink?

There are official guidelines.

There have been government guidelines on alcohol for adults for many years. They recommend that women should not regularly exceed 2–3 units daily and that men should not regularly exceed 3–4 units daily. However it wasn't until 2009 that the Chief Medical Officer for England and Wales issued guidelines on alcohol for under-18s and their parents.

The guidance says:[1]

- An alcohol-free childhood is best. Children shouldn't drink before they're 15.
- If 15 to 17 year-olds drink, it should only be once in a while and definitely no more than once a week.

- If 15 to 17 year-olds drink they should be supervised by a parent or other adult.
- Parents can have a big influence on their children's drinking.
- Support needs to be provided for young people who have alcohol-related problems and their parents.

The Scottish Government and Northern Ireland Executive both promote similar ideas.

But how can you get your children to stick to these guidelines? Read on for information and look out for practical advice in these speech bubbles.

[1] The Department of Health, '5 point plan for an alcohol free childhood' dh.gov.uk/en/News/Recentstories/DH_093912

Continue ▶

Activity 4

10 minutes

Consider the following B grade answer to the Activity 3 question and how it might be improved to an A grade answer to give more explicit explanation and interpretation of:

- how the image links to the audience and purpose
- how the image links to the other images earlier in the article
- how the image links to the text/headline cutting alongside it.

Add your ideas and improvements around the sample student answer below.

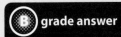

B grade answer

> The serious image on page 3 of the leaflet suggests that drinking has a negative effect on teenagers. The expression on his face and the plaster on his leg imply that the boy is unhappy and unhealthy. By showing a male teenager from an ethnic minority the image links to the wider implication of this leaflet that alcohol is not limited to one group of teenagers in society. The presentation of the headline cutting alongside this image shows that this teenager's activities are linked to the headline-grabbing issue of binge drinking in teenagers.

A
- ▶ Detailed response
- ▶ Material absorbed and shaped for purpose
- ▶ Good understanding of material

20 minutes

Return to your answer for Activity 3 on page 6.

Consider the grade criteria below and write an examiner comment and grade for your answer. Having looked at the grade criteria, what suggestions would you make to improve to your answer?

D
- ▶ Identifies two or more features
- ▶ Attempts to comment on both presentational and structural features
- ▶ Makes a statement about effectiveness

C
- ▶ Clear attempt to answer question
- ▶ Range of relevant points
- ▶ Both presentational and structural features covered
- ▶ Comments on presentational and structural features
- ▶ Comments on effectiveness

B
- ▶ Clear and effective attempt to answer question
- ▶ Range of relevant supported points
- ▶ Material firmly focused on presentational and structural features
- ▶ Some extended comments about effectiveness

A
- ▶ Detailed response
- ▶ Material absorbed and shaped for purpose
- ▶ Good understanding of material and effectiveness

A*
- ▶ Full, detailed, conceptualised response
- ▶ Material fully absorbed and shaped for purpose
- ▶ Full understanding of material and effectiveness

Examiner comment and grade:

Suggestions for improvement:

Skills to raise my grade

RAISE MY GRADE

Now that you have completed this lesson on audience and purpose, fill in the RAG table below to see if your confidence has improved.

	R	A	G
I can make inferences about the viewpoints conveyed in a text.	○	○	○
I can explain how the content of a text has been tailored to its audience and purpose.	○	○	○
I can identify what a text assumes and implies about its audience.	○	○	○
I can select relevant evidence to support my points.	○	○	○

Section A of the AQA GCSE English and English Language paper not only requires you to read and understand **three** different texts, but also to identify a viewpoint or viewpoints within a text. A writer will usually convey their own, or their organisation's viewpoint about a particular topic. They may also include others' viewpoints, that might differ from their own.

Beware of having an emotional response to an exam text. Examiners will choose topics that are of interest to people of your age. Sometimes students react too strongly to a topic that has some personal interest; remember only to answer the question you are asked and to support it with quotation rather than personal opinion. The subject matter of the text used in this lesson is a good example of this. As you read, note how far you could be distracted by your personal reaction to the material.

Definitions

Remind yourself of these terms and write definitions for each in the spaces provided.

Viewpoint:

Evidence:

What is PEE? Explain the practice of PEE for writing about a text you have read.

Skills to raise my grade

Fill in the RAG table below to show how confident you are in the following areas:

	R	A	G
I can confidently read and understand unseen texts.	○	○	○
I can interpret information and identify the viewpoint(s) being conveyed in a text.	○	○	○
I can select relevant quotations to support my points.	○	○	○
I can comment on and interpret those quotations.	○	○	○

20 minutes

Activity 1

1 Read the transcript of a speech given by Martin Narey, former Chief Executive of Barnardo's, about its Children in Trouble campaign.

Feral. Parasites. Vermin.

When did it start to become OK to talk about children like this? And why is it that the British public, who we polled, have such alarming views about children? 54 per cent of them thinking that children – all children – are beginning to behave like animals.

What can we do about it? What can we do about a public that overestimates not just a little bit, but by a factor of four, the amount of crime which young people commit?

Barnardo's is determined to address this. No other minority is casually spoken of in this appalling way. We need to change the public's view of children. We're not naïve; we work with a lot of difficult children, and children who commit crime or get involved with antisocial behaviour need to be made to face up to the reality of their actions. And, working with their schools and their families and the children themselves, we do that all over the UK.

But mostly, children in the UK are good; they volunteer in huge numbers, they help others, they are decent and they should not be spoken of in this way. Help us to change this appalling treatment of this key minority.

2 What is the TAPS of the transcript? (S = source, and is often useful to consider in addition to the text type, audience and purpose.)

T: _____

A: _____

P: _____

S: _____

3 Look at the statements below, which are jumbled up 'PEE' statements about Martin Narey's viewpoints in this speech.
- Identify which are points , evidence and explanations , by highlighting them using pink, yellow and green.
- Match relevant evidence and explanations to the points by drawing lines to link them up.
- Decide which PEE combination reflects the best quality answer. Mark the PEE with an asterisk (*) and give reasons for your choice in the space opposite.

'When did it start to become OK to talk about children like this?'

His use of the term 'children' rather than 'young people' or 'teenagers' is a suggestion that people are referring to a vulnerable or innocent group of people and his rhetorical question encourages the listener to consider the issue he raises and perhaps reconsider their own viewpoints on the topic.

This suggests that public viewpoints are inappropriate and unfair which is definitely the way many adults dismiss teenagers and cross the street to the other side just because they see boys wearing hoodies.

'But mostly children in the UK are good.'

He views the opinions of the UK public as concerning or even alarming.

This short statement emphasises his belief that a wrong is being done to children.

He thinks that the issue is urgent.

He refers to them as a 'key minority'.

He holds the view that the public, and most urgently the charity Barnardo's, should do something about this issue.

He uses the word 'appalling'.

His attitude is that the public's viewpoint on children is terrible.

His use of words such as 'feral' and 'wild' illustrate what he finds shocking.

The speaker disagrees with the widespread labelling of young people in negative terms.

His belief is that children who commit crimes should face up to their wrongs and that Barnardo's already support such work.

His belief is that the public's views on children must be changed to be more realistic.

His final statement shows that he believes children are important.

This both emphasises their role as the future of society and also suggests that they are easy targets for prejudice.

'We do that all over the UK.'

This reflects his belief that the British public are prejudiced because they are labelling a whole group of the population because of the behaviour of some.

His acknowledgement of this suggests that he does not want bad behaviour to be excused and emphasises that Barnardo's is making no excuses for those who do wrong.

'Barnardo's are determined to address this.'

Activity 2

5 minutes

Look at this photograph. What does it tell you about modern forms of bullying?

Activity 3

20 minutes

Read MP Vernon Coaker's speech in support of Anti-Bullying Week. Then answer these questions.

It's great to be here to support the national launch of Anti-Bullying Week 2009.

This is a very appropriate venue, because bullying, like the technology on show here at the Science Museum, moves with the times.

Just as the steam engine gave way to the internal combustion engine, so bullies have progressed from sticks and stones, and hurtful words, to cyberbullying.

And tackling cyberbullies is the theme of this year's Anti-Bullying Week. <u>It is a key part of our work to safeguard and ensure the well-being of all our children and young people.</u>

Modern technology allows us to keep in touch with old friends and make new ones. But it has also become a channel through which bullies operate.

Threats or abuse by email or text message are no different from spoken words. And when it is also possible to send images – to any number of people on a copy list – the damage can be even greater.

The slogan of this year's campaign is 'Stay safe in cyberspace'.

<u>Bullying, whether delivered with a word or a fist or a text message, can blight lives.</u> It can crush a young person's self-confidence, damage health and school performance, and cast a shadow over a whole future. In the most extreme cases, it can drive children to take desperate action when they can see no other way out.

So it's right that DCSF supports Anti-Bullying Week, and the work of the Anti-Bullying Alliance and Young ABA.

I'd like to pay tribute to the Anti-Bullying Alliance for all the wonderful work they are doing with schools and local authorities to raise awareness of bullying and how to tackle it.

Bullying can happen anywhere. But that also means it can be tackled anywhere. And the responsibility for stopping it lies with each one of us.

1   What is the TAP for this text?

T: _____

A: _____

P: _____

2   Look at the main viewpoints underlined in the text. Identify the supporting arguments made in the speech by underlining and annotating them.

If you laugh at someone who is being bullied, you help to create a bullying environment, and you put yourself on the side of the bully.

That is why DCSF is rerunning its 'Laugh at it and you're part of it' anti-cyberbullying campaign to coincide with Anti-Bullying Week. The aim of the campaign is to get people to think very carefully about the consequences of forwarding embarrassing images and emails.

We are also helping parents to talk to their children about bullying. A new online leaflet, 'Keep an eye on it' produced by ABA, Young ABA and NASUWT, provides information for parents and adults working with young people on how to spot the signs of bullying, and what they can do to help. It will give parents a better understanding of why bullying happens, what forms it takes, and what to do if their own children are being bullied.

Parents can also seek advice from Parentline Plus, funded by DCSF, which runs a helpline for parents whose children are being bullied, with trained advisors ready to offer advice, guidance and support. Parentline Plus also provides support through its 'Be Someone to Tell' website.

The Department's own 'Safe to Learn' guidance offers advice to schools on how to tackle bullying in general, as well as how they can respond to different kinds of bullying such as cyberbullying, homophobic bullying and racist bullying.

We know that when schools put the right policies in place, and work to create an environment where bullying is unacceptable, it stops. That's why we have given school staff stronger legal backing to confiscate mobile phones, and discipline pupils for bad behaviour outside the school gates. We have made it clear that any sort of bullying should not be tolerated, and must incur disciplinary sanctions.

Anti-Bullying Week is about taking this message out to the wider world: if you see bullying going on and you don't do anything about it, you are collaborating with it. Everyone has a responsibility to put a stop to bullying if they see it happening.

I have been really impressed by the creative and imaginative anti-bullying projects from around the country, often produced with the active involvement of young people themselves.

Projects such as the 'Speak, Stop, Solve' DVD produced by Yorkshire East Riding Youth Service; Winterton Comprehensive's anti-bullying presentation for other schools; the Cybermentors campaign from Beatbullying; and the artwork produced by young people from East Sussex.

I know that there is much other strong and effective work going on in every part of the UK.

What we need to remember is that if we act together, we are far stronger than the bullies. Thank you.

Activity 4

20 minutes

Choose **two** statements from the list below and add evidence and explanations to form PEE paragraphs in answer to the following question:

Comment on how Coaker crafts his language to convey his thoughts and feelings about bullying to his audience.

(8 marks)

Coaker uses figurative language (metaphor and simile) to outline his understanding of the modern and changing nature of bullying.

Coaker uses technical language to convey his knowledge of modern forms of communication and bullying.

Coaker uses proper nouns reflecting national organisations and activities linked to anti-bullying to demonstrate the government's awareness about anti-bullying action.

Coaker uses formal vocabulary and sentence structures appropriate for his audience to convey his argument about the importance of acting against bullying.

Coaker uses a variety of pronouns to reflect his own, the government's and his audience's viewpoints and engage his audience with his viewpoint.

PEE paragraph 1:

_____

_____

_____

_____

_____

PEE paragraph 2:

_____

_____

_____

_____

_____

_____

5 minutes

Activity 5

Annotate your PEE paragraphs from Activity 4 in line with your target grade from the criteria below. Mark up how you have met each of the criteria. Extend or edit your answer if you identify some weaknesses in your original paragraph.

- ▶ Offers detailed understanding and interpretation of the writer's viewpoint
- ▶ Shows detailed and perceptive appreciation, analysis and interpretation of how the writer has used language to convey viewpoint
- ▶ Offers full, relevant quotation to support ideas with appropriate and perceptive comments

- ▶ Offers clear evidence that the text is understood in relation to language
- ▶ Offers clear appreciation and analysis of the writer's choice of words and phrases to convey viewpoint
- ▶ Offers relevant and appropriate quotations to support ideas with appropriate comments

Look at the examiner comment on an A* answer to the exam question below. Then look at the B grade student answer. Identify the features needed to make this an A* answer (look back at the A* grade criteria on page 19). Can you write your own A* answer?

> Summarise Martin Narey's viewpoint and support this with quotation
> from the transcript.
>
> (8 marks)

A* examiner comment

The student's answer reflects the breadth of Narey's views on society and teenagers. Quotation is combined with comments and used precisely to illustrate perceptive reading, linking viewpoint to language choices.

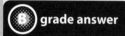

grade answer

Martin Narey's viewpoint in his speech is that people are being unfair to today's teenagers. He uses the example of the terms people use to describe teenagers:

"Feral. Parasites. Vermin". He is angry about this and this is clear by the vocabulary and imperatives he uses to insist people are wrong: "Help us to change this appalling treatment of this key minority."

Identifying the features needed to make this an A* answer

_____

_____

_____

_____

_____

_____

My A* answer

Skills to raise my grade

Now that you have completed this lesson on establishing meaning using supporting evidence and interpretation, fill in the RAG table below to see if your confidence has improved.

	R	A	G
I can confidently read and understand unseen texts.	○	○	○
I can interpret information and identify the viewpoint(s) being conveyed in a text.	○	○	○
I can select relevant quotations to support my points.	○	○	○
I can comment on and interpret those quotations.	○	○	○

One of the Reading questions in the exam paper will ask you to compare texts.

▶ You will need to plan your answer quickly and carefully. You will need to identify valid points of similarity and difference and ensure you write about **both** texts.

▶ To gain the very highest marks you need to demonstrate that you can distinguish subtle but important differences and prove these with evidence.

This lesson will help you in structuring comparative answers.

▶ It will give guidance on how to select and embed quotations in your answer.

▶ It will show you the areas of a text that offer potential for comparison. But the skills of insightful reading are ones that only you can be responsible for; you must read widely outside the classroom in preparation for the exam. One tip is to read some interesting newspaper and magazine stories from a variety of publications every week and notice their features as listed in the bullet points above.

RAISE MY GRADE

Skills to raise my grade

Fill in the RAG table below to show how confident you are in the following areas:

	R	A	G
I can compare two or more texts':			
• content	○	○	○
• audience	○	○	○
• purpose	○	○	○
• language features	○	○	○
• presentational and structural features.	○	○	○
I can select and cross-reference evidence to support my opinions on the above.	○	○	○
I can explain these comparisons with insight and perception.	○	○	○

Definitions

Remind yourself of the following terms and write a definition for each.

Compare:

_____

Collate:

_____

Language features:

_____

Presentational and structural features:

_____

_____

_____

Activity 1

10 minutes

1 Read the advert on page 24 and identify the TAPS.

T: _____

A: _____

P: _____

S: _____

2 Now annotate the language, presentational and structural features that you can identify in this advert.

Cadbury Dairy Milk Buttons: our little bags of fun turn fifty and Fairtrade

3 Fill in the table below with as many terms for language, presentational and structural features as you can. You can then use this for revision purposes before the final exam.

Language features	Presentational and structural features

Activity 2

15 minutes

1 Read the two extracts below and on page 26 and consider the following exam question.

Compare the ways language and grammar features are used in Texts 1 and 2. Give some examples and comment on their effect. **(16 marks)**

Text 1

Sun Sport 10 Nov 2007

Spurs to eat baby food

By ANTONY KASTRINAKIS

MEET Juande Ramos' secret weapon in his bid to turn Tottenham into world-beaters – **DOCTOR BABY FOOD.**

Antonio Escribano is in talks about joining Spurs' medical staff and bringing his magic mush with him.

Boss Ramos made a special request to bring in the University of Seville's professor to boost the fitness of Dimitar Berbatov and Co.

Escribano, 56, said: 'I will be there this weekend and we will talk to see how to arrange things. For me this is not a transfer – I will just be a medical consultant after the English club asked me.

'It's difficult for me to be there permanently because I am a professor in the university and I also work with five clubs in Spain. But if we can reach agreement it's no problem.'

Escribano, who worked with Ramos at Seville, is known as 'doctor baby food' in Spain because of his liquidised concoction of natural ingredients he gives players to aid their recovery after matches.

He added: 'The famous "baby food" is just a nutritional help at the end of matches and at half-time.

'It's good because it makes the recovery of the player much better.

'They have called me from England for my work and the one who called me is evidently Juande.

'I'm not annoyed that they know me as the man of the baby food. In reality it's just food.

'It was a Seville player that told me one day "this is what my baby eats" and people started calling it baby food. But it's really a drink.'

Text 2

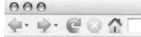

Guardian International

| Reviews | Comment | Sport | Culture | Business | Money |

Baby food giant hails hungry adult market

German firm Hipp says one in four consumers now grown-ups who find baby food easier to swallow and digest

Kate Connolly in Berlin
Friday 19 March 2010 17.55 GMT

Can't be bothered to chew your food? Too tired to cook and looking for a quick meal? It seems that in such circumstances a growing number of adults may consider opening a jar of baby food.

The world's largest baby food manufacturer, Hipp, has said an increasing number of adults are turning to its pre-cooked, pureed meals because they find them easier to swallow and digest.

About a quarter of those who eat the Bavaria-based firm's 100 varieties of pulped meals – from apple and cranberry breakfast to vegetable and beef hotpot – are adults, it says.

Claus Hipp said in recent years his firm's products had grown in popularity, particularly among elderly people, with stewed apple said to be a favourite.

He said the 50-year-old company – the world's largest producer of baby food, with 46% of the market – was increasingly turning its attention to the adult market rather than babies as Europe's population ages.

'Not so long ago, we had twice as many births as now, and that, of course, has a knock-on effect. As our society gets ever older, baby food is showing that it has a future in the adult market,' Hipp said at a company birthday celebration.

2 Now work out the TAP of each text.

Text 1 TAP:

T: _____

A: _____

P: _____

Despite the fact that birth rates have dropped in most European countries, most notably in Germany, the company's profits rose by €90m last year to €500m (£450m).

A million and a half jars of baby food come off the Hipp production line every day. Hipp said calorie-conscious new mothers saw the meals – which are low in fat, sugar and salt – as a way to help them lose weight after giving birth and were among new customers it had won in recent years. Sportsmen and women looking for a light meal are believed to favour the jars, too.

The company, which recommends its organic meals to babies 'at the start of weaning to three years of age', and makes no mention on its packaging of anyone above that age, said it had no intention of relaunching the products for a separate market.

'Older people can often cope with the mashed baby food better than regular meals, but we're not planning to change our advertising to target them … we want to keep our baby image,' said Hipp, whose father, Georg, started putting baby food in jars in 1960.

Eileen Steinbock, of the British Dietetic Association, said pureed food could benefit people whose ability to swallow had been greatly reduced through old age, dementia or a stroke, and was already in widespread use in care homes.

But people who could still chew and swallow should continue to do so for as long as possible, she added.

'I wouldn't like to see people being given pureed food just because it's easier for a carer to give it to them that way. It should only be given when it's appropriate or essential,' she said.

In addition, the protein content of food declines when it is pureed because extra water is added to help liquefy it, leaving it with fewer calories. 'That would be a bad thing because a lot of people who require pureed food find it hard to eat enough and are quite likely to be nutritionally compromised and possibly even malnourished,' she added.

Text 2 TAP:

T: _____

A: _____

P: _____

27

20 minutes

Activity 3

1 a Annotate Text 1 on page 25, underlining all the language and grammar features you can identify.

   b List main language techniques used by the author, remembering to use the Point Evidence Explanation format.

- P: _____

  _____

  E: _____

  E: _____

  _____

- P: _____

  _____

  E: _____

  E: _____

  _____

- P: _____

  _____

  E: _____

  E: _____

  _____

- P: _____

  _____

  E: _____

  E: _____

  _____

2 Annotate Text 2 on pages 26–27 and create four PEE bullet points on language and grammar in the same way as you did for Text 1.

- P: _____

  _____

  E: _____

  E: _____

  _____

- P: _____

  _____

  E: _____

  E: _____

  _____

- P: _____

  _____

  E: _____

  E: _____

  _____

- P: _____

  _____

  E: _____

  E: _____

  _____

3 Identify the similarities and differences in language features between the two texts, using the planning format below:

Text 1

Similarities

Text 2

15 minutes

Activity 4

Answer the examination question from Activity 2:

Compare the ways language and grammar features are used in Texts 1 and 2. Give some examples and comment on their effect. **(16 marks)**

Activity 5

Incorporate the following features into the student answer below to raise it to an A grade answer.

A

▶ Use of brief embedded quotation
▶ Use of connectives for comparison
▶ Perceptive appreciation shown of how and why the writer uses language techniques
▶ Cross referencing and comparison demonstrated throughout the answer

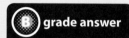
B grade answer

The Sun text is more reliant on simple and compound sentences. Paragraph 2 is made up of a compound sentence conveying information about the doctor and his product. This simply and easy writing style is appropriate for the Sun readers of the sport section. The Guardian text makes more use of more complex sentence structures, using hypens to mark subclauses for example in paragraph 5 and 7 where further information is given about the relationship between higher sales and falling birth rates: 'Despite the fact that birth rates have dropped in most European countries, most notably in Germany, the company's profits rose by 90m last year to 500m.' This links well to the Guardian audience who are expecting a more detailed and challenging article.

The Guardian text offers more specific and factual information than the Sun. For example, statistics about how many varieties of meal Hipp produce, company profits and daily production figures are quoted in the article. 'Despite the fact that birth rates have droppe in most European countries, most notably in Germany, the company's profits rose by 90m last year to 500m.' The Sun article is more vague and general in its language. One example of this is at the beginning when it talks about the doctor 'being in talks' with Spurs which means that the doctor being linked to the team is only a possibility rather than a reality. This doesn't quite tie in with the headline of the article.

You will now have an opportunity to revisit the exam-style answer that you wrote in Activity 4 (page 31), comparing the two texts.

Consider the grade criteria below and highlight the parts of your answer that reflect your target grade.

 D
- ▶ Identifies two or more features
- ▶ Comments on both language and grammar features
- ▶ Attempts to compare

 C
- ▶ Clear attempt to answer the question
- ▶ Several relevant points
- ▶ Both language and grammar features covered
- ▶ One clear supported comparison

 B
- ▶ Clear and successful attempt to answer question
- ▶ Range of relevant points about uses
- ▶ Both language and grammar features well covered
- ▶ Two or more supported comparisons

 A
- ▶ Full and detailed grasp of language and grammar
- ▶ Uses clearly linked to examples
- ▶ Material absorbed and shaped for purpose
- ▶ Range of clear comparisons

 A*
- ▶ Full, detailed, conceptualised comparisons of uses
- ▶ Material fully absorbed and shaped for purpose
- ▶ Full understanding of the material

Have you achieved your target grade? If not, write down how you could improve your answer to get that target grade.

Suggestions for improvement

_____

_____

_____

_____

_____

_____

_____

_____

_____

_____

_____

Skills to raise my grade

Now that you have completed this lesson on comparing and cross-referencing texts, fill in the RAG table below to see if your confidence has improved.

	R	A	G
I can compare two or more texts':			
• content	○	○	○
• audience	○	○	○
• purpose	○	○	○
• language features	○	○	○
• presentational and structural features.	○	○	○
I can select and cross-reference evidence to support my opinions on the above.	○	○	○
I can explain these comparisons with insight and perception.	○	○	○

4H Organising your ideas for writing

Skills you need ▶

You must show that you can:
- Plan your writing
- Sequence information in paragraphs and as a complete text

You will have discussed the planning of Writing answers in your English lessons, but despite the importance of this, many students still fail to discipline themselves to do this in the exam.

The planning stage of writing is **crucial** for your success in the exam. An assured piece of writing has to be dynamic from beginning to end; it needs to have a strong opening and a strong conclusion. It needs to have distinct points that build to form a cohesive viewpoint. Planning is vital for this.

This lesson will focus on how to plan and order your points in response to a Writing question. It will support you in using a plan to make sure you paragraph your writing properly.

RAISE MY GRADE

Skills to raise my grade

Fill in the RAG table below to show how confident you are in the following areas:

	R	A	G
I can plan a series of points.	○	○	○
I discipline myself **always** to make a plan before I write.	○	○	○
I can sequence my planned points in a logical order.	○	○	○
I can structure and paragraph my writing to reflect my plan.	○	○	○

10 minutes

Activity 1

1 Read the press report on the Government's policy on 5 hours of sport in schools on pages 37–38.

FIVE HOURS OF SPORT A WEEK FOR EVERY CHILD

£100m CAMPAIGN, ANNUAL NATIONAL SCHOOL SPORTS WEEK ANNOUNCED

A £100m campaign to give every child the chance of five hours of sport every week was announced by the Prime Minister, Gordon Brown today.

He called for a 'united team effort' in the run up to 2012 to make sport a part of every child's day to build a greater sporting nation and a fitter nation. He wants schools, parents, volunteers, coaches and the sports world to offer the equivalent of an hour of sport to every child, every day of the school week.

The plans include greater emphasis on competition within and between schools, a network of competition managers and a new National School Sports Week.

The new funding will provide:

- up to five hours of sport per week for all pupils, including two hours within the curriculum, and three hours for young people aged 16–19

- a new National School Sport Week, championed by Dame Kelly Holmes where all schools will be encouraged to run sports days and inter-school tournaments. This will build on the success of the UK School Games and its impact on motivating young people to take part in competitive sport

- a network of 225 competition managers across the country to work with primary and secondary schools to increase the amount of competitive sport they offer

- more coaches in schools and the community to deliver expert sporting advice to young people.

The Government will also challenge the sporting bodies to develop modern school sport competitions leading to local, regional and national finals.

The new funding builds on the £633 million already committed to creating a world-class school sport and PE system over the next three years.

The Prime Minister said:

'We need to put school sport back where it belongs, playing a central role in the school day. I was lucky enough to have primary and secondary schools that had sport at the centre of their ethos. I want every child to have that opportunity to take part.

'Watching sport is a national pastime. Talking about sport is a national obsession. But now we need to make taking part in sport a national characteristic.

'Whatever their natural ability and whatever their age, sport and activity can make our children healthier, raise self-confidence and self-esteem. It develops teamwork, discipline and a sense of fair play. Values that will stand young people and the country in good stead in the years to come.

▶

'To do this will take a concerted campaign, a real team effort. Government is doing its bit. Schools, parents, volunteers and the sporting world can do theirs. I call on them to join us. Together we can help every child be the best they can be.'

The moves will help strengthen the competitive framework for school sport – from grassroots to elite. The ultimate aim is for every child to have access to a range of sporting competition from local and regional level, leading on to national finals.

Mr Brown announced the campaign today at a visit to the West London Academy with culture secretary James Purnell and children schools and families secretary Ed Balls. The school, in Ealing, has an excellent reputation for competitive sport and for its PE provision, for both its own pupils and for those from its partner schools.

Mr Purnell said:

'Competitive sport is enjoyable and good for all children and young people, not just those who excel. It helps improve children's teamwork and social skills, and boosts confidence and self esteem. Competitive sport gives every child the chance to be the very best they can be and help us find the champions of tomorrow.

'Many schools are already committed to competitive sport, but often focused on the school's top athletes. We want every child, in every school, to have the opportunity to compete. We want to see a return to competitions within school as well as a healthy rivalry between schools. Competitive sport should be a key part of school life.'

Mr Balls said:

'There has been a quiet revolution in school sport in the past few years. This new package of measures builds on the hugely successful national strategy for PE and school sport and aims to deliver a world class system for PE and school sport for all our young people. The creation of a national competition framework, the increase in the number of professional coaches and the extension of increased sporting opportunities to many more young people than before will all help to keep this country at the forefront of school sport provision and get more young people thinking about their own health and wellbeing.'

Double Olympic Champion Dame Kelly Holmes said:

'In my role as National School Sport Champion, I've seen a lot of great work going on in schools across the country to encourage more young people to get involved in playing and taking part in competitive sport, and that's why the added investment announced by the Government today is a welcome boost. It will enable more schools to offer more competitive sport to their pupils helping more of them to achieve their potential. I therefore welcome the launch of a national school sport week, which will further enhance these opportunities.'

2   Rank the three openings on page 39 to the question below in order of merit. The best answer should have the following:
   - an arresting, interesting start
   - appropriate register (formal/informal)
   - a clear link to the question
   - clarity for the reader/examiner about the audience and purpose of the text.

Write a letter from a teenager to the Schools Minister, arguing for or against the policy of 5 hours of sport a week.   **(24 marks)**

Student	Letter opening	Rank
Student A	I am writing to express my concern on reading your recent press release about 5 hours compulsory PE in schools. As a 15-year-old teenage boy who has never excelled in this area, this seems to me another example of the 'nanny state' and will offer yet another opportunity to be publically shamed by my incompetence in this area.	
Student B	Marathons and multi gyms? Mountain biking and martial arts? Well give me a mars bar and a lucozade any day, but forget the physical exertion! Is it not time that young people should be able to make up their own minds about what is good for them and how they want to live their lives?	
Student C	It is about time that you did something about the growing obesity in young people today. Reports show that many children are not doing enough exercise. Its time now that things should change and it is the job of schools and parents to change things.	

10 minutes

Activity 2

1   What is the TAP required by the question in Activity 1?

T: _____

A: _____

P: _____

2   Plan possible points for a letter that supports the Schools Minister's policy.
Jot down a spider diagram below. Remember to make distinct points which
you will be able to extend and justify with evidence/argument.

Activity 3

15 minutes

1 Look at the statements below. Link any points that are similar or repetitive. Then reword them into **five** clearly expressed points of argument: **two** that acknowledge the opposing viewpoint, and **three** that come down in support of the policy. Use the diagram on page 41 to record this as a plan.

We are already doing more sport in schools than we were in 2008.

There is little enough time in schools to get through the requirements of GCSEs without adding more to lesson time.

There is not enough time for more PE in schools.

Today's children are just not fit enough and parents and schools need to do something about it.

Good health will have an impact on behaviour in schools.

Healthy children means happy children.

It is important to establish children having a lifelong love of sport.

Friendly competition is an important part of sport and an important part of life.

Sport can be offered not only in the curriculum but also for extra curricular or extended schools offerings.

Children today are less active than children of previous generations.

Obesity is an increasing problem in the UK so we need to begin a focus on health and fitness early in life.

Sport can give non-academic children an area in which to excel and gain respect.

Today's computer-generation children are becoming couch potatoes.

Points in favour
of the policy

•

•

•

**Write a letter from a teenager
to the Schools Minister, arguing
for or against the policy of 5 hours
of sport a week.**

Points against
the policy

•

•

•

_____

_____

_____

_____

_____

_____

_____

_____

_____

2 Now write your own plan along the same lines, arguing **against** the policy. In line with the modelling above, you should compose a long list of points, and then consider producing a five-point plan.

Activity 4

20 minutes

Now answer the exam-style question below using the plan you completed for Activity 3.

Write a letter from a teenager to the Schools Minister, arguing against the policy of 5 hours of sport a week.

(24 marks)

Continue ▶

Continue ▶

_____

_____

_____

_____

_____

_____

Activity 5

10 minutes

Look at the 'organisation of ideas' grade criteria below.

A*
- ▶ Form, content and style assuredly matched to purpose and audience
- ▶ Controlled and sustained crafting
- ▶ Highly effective and delightful vocabulary choices
- ▶ Distinctive and consistently effective

Have you addressed all of these points in your writing?

Look at your answer to Activity 4 in the light of these criteria and annotate one or two paragraphs with the changes you would make in order to raise your grade to an A*.

Activity 6

5 minutes

Fill in the table below to create a word bank, containing words and phrases from your writing and from the A* GradeStudio text on page 46 for use in argument and persuasion.

Words/phrases to argue/persuade

Read the conclusions from two student responses to the exam question below, together with the examiner comments. Then complete the Tips and practice section opposite.

> Write a letter from a teenager to the Schools Minister, arguing against the policy of 5 hours of sport a week.
>
> (24 marks)

B grade answer

Student B

> It is also important to remember that we should all have free choice. This is an important viewpoint in our country. It is important for the adults to practice what they preach and not be hypocritical by forcing activities on us that they cannot do themselves. It's just adults bossing you around. Perhaps you could think of advising young people rather than imposing things on us. You never know, with gentle but persuasive advice, maybe we would come to these activities ourselves, without it being forced on us.

Annotations:
- Lapse into informal style
- Effective vocabulary of argument
- Repetitive vocabulary
- Valid point of argument
- Weakness in subject–verb agreement

Examiner comment

This is a generally secure attempt with relevant material to the topic that is argued successfully. Sentences are generally secure though a wider variety of punctuation is required. Some of the writing is appropriately formal couched in well-chosen vocabulary, but this is not maintained throughout.

A* grade answer

Student A

> In summary, therefore, I'm sure you'll agree that there can be no justification for imposing activities that will not only present a hindrance to academic progress in schools, but also provide an arena for bullying of those students who cannot excel in physical activity. I would ask you to reconsider your viewpoint on this matter and take notice of the voice of the young people whom you should also represent. While your namesake, the former Arsenal Player Ian Wright would I'm sure agree with you in being keen on sport in schools, he was also involved in the TV programme 'What kids really think'. Perhaps you have forgotten to ask the people that really matter in all this – the people that can make a real difference – the young people of today.

Annotations:
- Material appropriate for a conclusion
- Argumentative/persuasive marker
- Correctly assertive/argumentative
- Appropriate summary of the main arguments presented in the body of the text
- Appropriate use of imperatives to argue
- Well reasoned
- Neatly structured concluding line that is both challenging and appropriately formal

Examiner comment

This is an assured piece which demonstrates a keen awareness of audience and purpose and is appropriately formal in register. The student uses a wide variety of vocabulary and summarises the arguments in the piece lucidly. The letter ends neatly with a variety of persuasive and thought provoking appeals, while giving reference to real-world sporting heroes.

Tips and practice

Write down or discuss what you have learnt about:

Openings: _____

_____

Endings: _____

_____

Paragraphing: _____

_____

Planning: _____

_____

Now you can apply what you have learnt to all your writing practice.

1 Plan your points.
2 Sequence your ideas.
3 Ensure your openings and endings are arresting and make explicit links to the key words in the title.

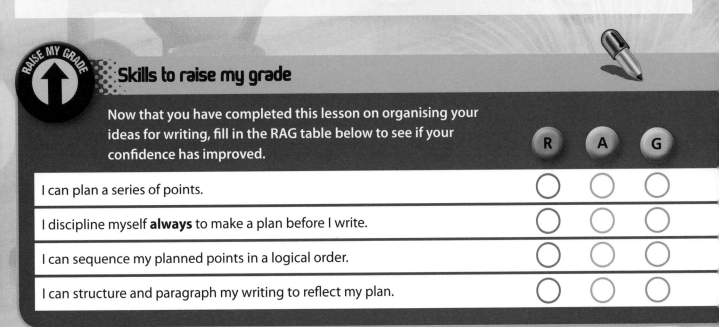

Skills to raise my grade

RAISE MY GRADE

Now that you have completed this lesson on organising your ideas for writing, fill in the RAG table below to see if your confidence has improved.

	R	A	G
I can plan a series of points.	○	○	○
I discipline myself **always** to make a plan before I write.	○	○	○
I can sequence my planned points in a logical order.	○	○	○
I can structure and paragraph my writing to reflect my plan.	○	○	○

Skills you need ▷

You must show that you can:
- Write in secure sentences
- Use simple, compound, complex and minor sentences for effect
- Use a range of vocabulary for effect

To achieve the highest grades in Writing questions you must demonstrate that you have mastery over the range of sentence types and vocabulary you use in your writing. You need to show that you use a variety of sentence types and that you do this **consciously** (on purpose) to achieve certain effects. Examples might be: use short sentences to create impact; follow short sentences with a longer complex sentence to create variety and interest for your reader.

In this lesson you will:

▷ revise the different sentence types that you will have been taught during your English course

▷ look at a model of writing where the author uses a variety of sentence structures to achieve particular effects

▷ put what you have seen into practice in your own writing.

RAISE MY GRADE ↑ Skills to raise my grade

Fill in the RAG table below to show how confident you are in the following areas:

	R	A	G
I can consistently write in sentences that are complete and grammatically correct.	○	○	○
I understand the terms simple, complex, compound and minor sentences.	○	○	○
I can write in simple, complex, compound and minor sentences.	○	○	○
I can choose sentence types to achieve particular effects in my writing.	○	○	○
I can choose vocabulary to create particular effects in my writing.	○	○	○

Activity 1

5 minutes

Look at the image below. Fill in the two word bank boxes below focusing on:
- language to convey the senses
- specialist terms that might be used in writing linked with this image.

Senses

Specialist terms

Activity 2

5 minutes

Read the article below, which is an extract from a longer article. As you read, underline:

- any descriptive/entertaining language
- specialist/informative vocabulary.

Before you begin work, make sure you have identified the TAP of this text:

T: _____

A: _____

P: _____

| Reviews | Comment | Sport | Travel | Business | Money | Lifestyle | Blogs |

Guardiantravel
Shark tales in South Africa

Scuba-diving with sharks in the Indian Ocean south of Durban, protected by just a mask and a wetsuit, rather than a steel cage.

I placed my mask over my face and checked the regulator. We had made it from the beach through the big surf – it was a rough day – and were now four miles off the South African coast, sitting on the gunwales of an inflatable dive boat that was rising and falling through two metres or more every few seconds.

'Remember,' said Kenny, one of the instructors, 'I'm your dive buddy – you stay with me. OK? If we see sharks, we remain calm, we stay upright in the water, we give them space.'

There is something quite comforting about the steady suck and hiss of Scuba apparatus. Your breathing slows and becomes regular. You are separated from the world by a sheet of glass. You get that irrational feeling of safety that a mosquito net can bring in man-eating lion territory.

And we were in man-eater country. The Indian Ocean coast of South Africa saw 86 shark attacks between 1992 and 2008, with 11 fatalities. Before the trip I went through the species of shark in my copy of *Sea Fishes of Southern Africa*, noting their characteristics: 'may threaten divers', 'positively linked to attacks on humans', 'voracious predator' – the word 'aggressive' came up time and again.

In Cape Town there is a much publicised thrill available whereby divers are lowered in a steel cage with some bait. Sharks then attack. Sharks, after all, are fiendishly dangerous. They are demons for a secular age. Even snakes have a better reputation.

Nigel Pickering, however, disagrees with all the demonisation. A former police diver from England, he came out to South Africa with his wife, Lesley, in 2003 and chose to live in the small and leafy town of Umkomaas, 25 miles south of Durban on the KwaZulu-Natal coast. Umkomaas is a quiet, amiable sort of place with a few good restaurants and bars on a long stretch of sandy shoreline. Nigel and Lesley set up their dive school in a handsome clapboard building with bright comfortable rooms for divers to stay in. There was, however, one other major attraction that drew Nigel to this coast: sharks. About four miles offshore, in the impressively muscular ocean, is a shallow area known as Aliwal Shoal. It is regularly listed among the world's top dive sites, being home to myriad sea creatures, including several species of shark. And Nigel is on a mission when it comes to sharks.

Diving with a ragged-tooth shark on Aliwal Shoal, South Africa. *Photograph: Alamy*

10 minutes

Activity 3

1 Complete the table below by writing your own examples of a simple, complex, compound and minor sentence.

Simple sentence	Minor sentence	Compound sentence	Complex sentence
I feel happy.	Happiness!	I feel happy and I am doing well at school.	I feel happy because I'm doing well at school.

2 a Look at the annotated version of paragraph 2 from the article. Read comments on the use of sentence types in relation to the audience and purpose of the text.

> Compound sentence giving information using specialist terminology associated with diving

I placed my mask over my face and checked the regulator. We had made it from the beach through the big surf – it was a rough day – and were now four miles off the South African coast, sitting on the gunwales of an inflatable dive boat that was rising and falling through two metres or more every few seconds.

> Complex sentence giving information about who, when, where of the travel article. Hyphens are used to create a parenthetical clause in order to create excitement and atmosphere to engage the reader in the excitement and danger of the activity

b Select **two** sentences from the remaining text where you can see the writer has consciously chosen the sentence type for effect. Justify the reasons for your choice.

Sentence 1:

_____

_____

_____

_____

_____

_____

_____

Sentence 2:

_____

_____

_____

_____

_____

_____

_____

Activity 4

20 minutes

1 What is the TAP of the answer required by the following exam-style question?

> **Describe a place that has made a strong impression on you, either positive or negative. Explain the reasons for your choice and convey a strong sense of that place to your reader.** **(16 marks)**

T: _____

A: _____

P: _____

2 Now fill in the word bank below in relation to the Text type, Audience and Purpose you have identified. This will form a plan for the Writing question.

Text type: _____	Audience: _____	Purpose: _____

3 Write your answer to the question, using your plan.

Activity 5

5 minutes

1 Annotate your answer to Activity 4 to identify **three** different sentence types and **three** examples of engaging vocabulary.

2 Now note down your successes and areas for improvement:

Successes:

Areas for improvement:

Activity 6

RAISE MY GRADE

10 minutes

Look at the extract from a B grade answer below to the question in Activity 4, page 52. Annotate it with the improvements you would make to raise it to an A grade.

B grade answer

> London. Ever been there? Or are you looking to go there? Well don't!
>
> The jigsaw of Hackney is made up of pieces of separate little estates. Each of them is like an empire of its own. Each has their own rules and each has their own rulers and workers. You walk through them at night and there are hoodies on most corners. Quiet. Murder. The only muttered conversation is if someone is robbing you or saying something intimidating.

A
▶ Effective range of vocabulary choices
▶ Uses full range of sentence structures accurately

Here are extracts from two student responses to the question in Activity 4:

> Describe a place that has made a strong impression on you, either positive or negative. Explain the reasons for your choice and convey a strong sense of that place to your reader.
>
> (16 marks)

Read the answers below and on page 56 and then try to match the examiner comments that follow with the correct student response.

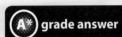

A* grade answer

Student A

Unforgettable.

Holy cows in the middle of the road chewing on what they can find in rubbish bins. Cars circling them with horns blaring. Rickshaws with men driving them and laughing as if possessed by the chaos. India is a once in a lifetime experience, but you take that life in your hands.

For years my family stalled about taking me, with a variety of excuses. 'Mosquitoes will bite you', dismissed my father. 'I can't take the heat,' muttered my mother.

But eventually, they relented. After all, it's in my blood.

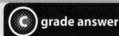

C grade answer

Student B

Awareness of audience and purpose establishing setting in relation to the title

Attempt to create atmosphere with additional descriptive detail

Words describing the men and women reflect developed vocabulary

The local park is a depressing place. It's meant to be a park for children and families and it's used by them in the day. Old men sit around chatting on park benches, moaning. Mums with lots of children sit on benches chatting and not really watching what their children are doing. And children are running round where there are bits of broken glass and equipments that have peeling paint and are not always working properly.

Short simple sentence followed by minor and complex sentences provide variety

Minor sentence for effect

It's at night that the problems start. Shadows. Quiet spooky paths through the trees. Groups of teenagers from the community college sit in the children's playground where they are not allowed to be. It's the teenagers, drinking and playing on the equipment that's too small for them, that make problems that are left for the daytime. You can't walk through the park if you're not one of their gang without one of them shouting something at you.

Examiner comment 1

The student engages the reader with detailed and developed description. A variety of vocabulary is used including specialist and descriptive vocabulary. All sentence types are used including a one sentence paragraph

Examiner comment 2

There are three different kinds of sentence here, all securely and accurately marked out.
Vocabulary is reasonably varied and used consciously to create an atmosphere.

Student A matches examiner comment _____

Student B matches examiner comment _____

Tips and practice

Tips

Write down or discuss what you have learnt about:

Varying sentences: _____

_____

Varying vocabulary: _____

_____

Practice

Now apply what you have learnt to all your writing practice.

1 Check that you have used at least **one** of each form and are not relying on one sort of sentence type throughout your writing.

2 Create a word bank.

3 Check that you have used a variety of vocabulary linked to your audience and purpose.

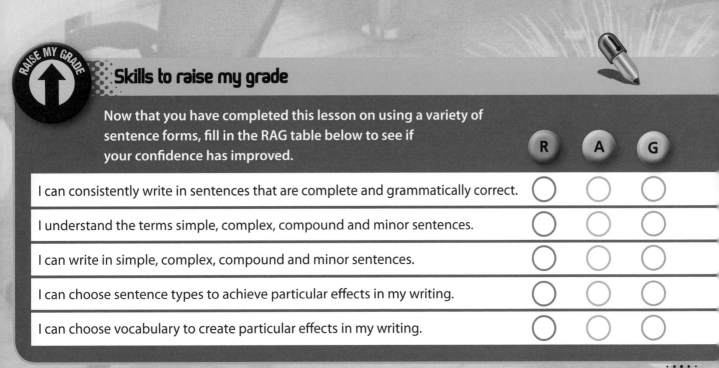

Skills to raise my grade

Now that you have completed this lesson on using a variety of sentence forms, fill in the RAG table below to see if your confidence has improved.

	R	A	G
I can consistently write in sentences that are complete and grammatically correct.	○	○	○
I understand the terms simple, complex, compound and minor sentences.	○	○	○
I can write in simple, complex, compound and minor sentences.	○	○	○
I can choose sentence types to achieve particular effects in my writing.	○	○	○
I can choose vocabulary to create particular effects in my writing.	○	○	○

You will have been taught how to use a variety of punctuation marks. However, many students forget to demonstrate this in the exam. Demonstrating your confidence with a variety of punctuation is crucial to achieving a C grade and above. Examiners can only mark what they see, so it's important that you show them the range of what you know.

Once you have finished writing, proofread your work and check that you have demonstrated a variety of punctuation marks. Beware of using too many of the same punctuation marks; for example, lots of candidates overuse the exclamation mark. Make sure that you are confident with the rules behind using semi colons and colons. This is an area that many adults continue to lack confidence with in later life, so now is a good time to secure your knowledge!

This lesson will revise how to use a variety of punctuation marks. It will support you in practising how to use them.

RAISE MY GRADE

Skills to raise my grade

Fill in the RAG table below to show how confident you are in the following areas:	R	A	G
I can use commas, full stops, question marks, ellipses and exclamation marks.	○	○	○
I can punctuate direct speech correctly.	○	○	○
I can use colons and semi colons.	○	○	○
I remember to use a variety of punctuation marks in my writing.	○	○	○

Activity 1

10 minutes

Fill in the table below.

Punctuation mark	
Full stop	
Inverted commas	
Quote marks	
Comma	
Apostrophe	
Question mark	
Exclamation mark	
Colon	
Semi colon	
Ellipsis	

Activity 2

10 minutes

1 Look at this advert from the Autism Trust featuring the charity's founder, Polly Tommey.

Hello Boys.
Autism is worth over 6 million votes.
It's time to talk ...

Polly Tommey

the autism trust

www.theautismtrust.org.uk

2 Identify the punctuation marks used in the advert and explain why they have been used.

1   Punctuation mark: _____   Purpose: _____

2   Punctuation mark: _____   Purpose: _____

3   Punctuation mark: _____   Purpose: _____

Activity 3

15 minutes

1 Read the Autism Trust Press release which accompanied the advert shown in Activity 2.

Polly Tommey's Campaign Continues...
Labour Party first to respond.

Last week Polly Tommey sent letters to the three main party leaders urging them to talk to her about autism in the UK and the action needed. Yesterday the Labour Party responded with an invitation to discuss how they can help the autism community. Tomorrow, Polly will go to Downing Street to do just that.

Polly says, 'The Labour Party have not underestimated the power of the autism community. With over 6 million votes and the current likelihood of a hung parliament, it really is in the interest of the party leaders to come forward with some concrete policies to encourage our vote; we have the power to determine the general election outcome.'

Polly's billboards will be displayed from Monday 29th March in London's most viewed digital billboard locations, as well as multiple locations throughout the UK.

2 Write an alternative slogan for the campaign, using the punctuation marks discussed in Activity 2.

_____

_____

_____

25 minutes

Activity 4

1 Identify the TAP required by an answer to this exam question.

> **Write a letter of complaint or support to the Autism Trust in reaction to Tommey's provocative ad campaign. Explain the reasons for your viewpoint and argue your case for or against the advert.**
>
> **(16 marks)**

T: _____

A: _____

P: _____

2 Now answer the question, making sure you use at least **one** example of each of the punctuation marks discussed in Activity 1. You can tick them off in the table below.

Full stop		Question mark	
Inverted commas		Exclamation mark	
Quote marks		Colon	
Comma		Semi colon	
Apostrophe		Ellipsis	

_____

_____

_____

_____

_____

_____

_____

_____

_____

_____

_____

Continue ▶

Continue ▸

Activity 5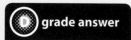

 15 minutes

Read this extract from a D grade answer to the exam question. Annotate the answer to improve it by correcting the punctuation errors.

D grade answer

I am writing to support Polly Tommey and her brave work for

your autism advert what proves that she has done the right

thing is that the three leader's have all been in contact with her

to discuss autism as a result of the ad! I have a brother with

autism and knowing exactly the effect of this on the family and

the stress that people with the condition and their families

have and how there has not been enough attention given to this

issue. If the only way to get attention of the people in power is

to be provocative then why not, it's the twenty first century

and we don't live like Victorian's any more! As Polly herself said

'many parent's of autistic children would take off their clothes

and run round the park naked if it got the attention of the

people in power to do something about this important issue!'

GradeStudio

Here are extracts from two student responses to the question in Activity 4, page 61:

> Write a letter of complaint or support to the Autism Trust in reaction to Tommey's provocative ad campaign. Explain the reasons for your viewpoint and argue your case for or against the advert.
>
> (16 marks)

1 Read the answers below and on page 66 together with the examiner comments.

A* grade answer

Student A

Dear Ms Tommey,

I am writing to express my disgust at the recent tactics of the Autism Trust to gain political and media attention. I have been, for some time, an active supporter of the society and recognise the value of your work for autistic people. However, I cannot condone what I can only regard as sleazy, low-brow exploitation of female sexuality to gain attention.

The image used on the billboard, aimed at the three political party leaders for the 2010 elections, is shocking…and for all the wrong reasons. Today is the 21st century! Bras were burnt in the 60s; surely now is not the time for using them to get attention from those in power?

Can I urge you to consider the impact of your tactics on today's young people? Horrific! We are already battling with the 'culture of pink' and the sexualisation of primary age girls by commercial organisations: perfumes for girls, sexy underwear for junior school children, Barbie make up lines and glitter everywhere. What next?

Commas used for parenthesis

Use of ellipsis to create pause

Effective use of rhetorical question for writing to argue

Use of exclamation for effect

Examiner comment

The candidate writes in an assured and appropriately formal style. A variety of linguistic devices are employed, such as pauses and rhetorical questions. These are well-supported with a range of punctuation.

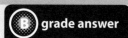

GradeStudio

Student B

> Dear Sir/Madam,
>
> I am writing about your billboard that I spotted today in London's Marble Arch. I must say I am very disturbed by your old fashioned views that are displayed there. Maybe you could say this is a joke, but after the protests of many women in the last 50 years, there is no excuse for using images of women's bodies for cheap political reasons!
>
> Cheap! Nasty! Low! These words describe your advert! In future, you should fight your battles through issues rather than by putting down women. I am surprised at the poor choice of your charity. This does women no favours. I will certainly no longer be supporting your fundraising work.

Use of exclamation for effect

Use of exclamation mark – rather overused

Examiner comment

The candidate's work adopts an appropriate register for argument, though at times veers towards informal structures and vocabulary. A range of simple punctuation is used consciously for effect. Points of argument are valid but could be more tightly planned and structured.

2   Now write down **five** examiner tips for students answering this question, before completing the Tips and practice section opposite.

Examiner tips:

- _____
- _____
- _____
- _____
- _____

Tips and practice

Tips

Write down or discuss what you have learnt about:

The rules of punctuation: _____

_____

Using a variety of punctuation marks: _____

_____

Practice

Now apply what you have learnt to all your writing practice.

1 Check that you have used a variety of punctuation marks and not overused any of the less common marks such as exclamation marks.

2 Ensure that you have used an example of more complex punctuation such as a semi colon and colon.

RAISE MY GRADE

Skills to raise my grade

Now that you have completed this lesson on using a variety of punctuation, fill in the RAG table below to see if your confidence has improved.

	R	A	G
I can use commas, full stops, question marks, ellipses and exclamation marks.	◯	◯	◯
I can punctuate direct speech correctly.	◯	◯	◯
I can use colons and semi colons.	◯	◯	◯
I remember to use a variety of punctuation marks in my writing.	◯	◯	◯

When it comes to the final exam, there are two skills that students often forget in the panic to write an answer in time-restricted conditions: planning (covered in lesson 4H) and proofreading. You will undoubtedly have been reminded to proofread your work by your teacher. This is not the most exciting part of writing, but it can be the difference between gaining or losing a grade.

Even some of the most confident students are prone to repeated patterns of error in their writing. Make sure that you have identified your weaknesses and know your related targets, as highlighted by your mocks or other practice papers. If you are not sure about these, have a discussion with your teacher. In exam conditions, try to proofread by 'reading aloud in your head' in the exam, to 'hear' what you have written.

This lesson allows you to practise your proofreading skills. It demonstrates some of the common mistakes students make. It supports you in planning time for proofreading in the final exam.

RAISE MY GRADE

Skills to raise my grade

Fill in the RAG table below to show how confident you are in the following areas:	R	A	G
I can recognise when sentences are secure or insecure.	○	○	○
I can use a range of punctuation accurately.	○	○	○
I can use a range of vocabulary that is accurately spelt.	○	○	○
I always proofread my written work.	○	○	○

Common problems with sentences

▶ Comma splicing: dividing sentences with a comma rather than a full stop or equivalent

Barbados has unspoilt beaches and a lively nightlife, on the island you will find something for all the family.

▶ No finite verb

Lying in the heat of the sun, the water lapping at my feet and a cocktail on the table next to me.

▶ Tense not maintained

it was the best holiday of my life and Eleanor will be able to come with me

Subject–verb agreement

Our hotel, famous for its friendliness and charm, welcome children and animals.

General sentence sense

The animals, looking through the cages, we all felt badly though knowing it's not right.

Activity 1

20 minutes

Read the sentences below. Highlight secure sentences in yellow. Highlight insecure sentences in pink, annotating each with a reason for your decision. Rewrite the sentences that need improving in the spaces given.

It will be a dream holiday, firstly I attended all rides and have the time of my life.

_____

_____

In the side of the blue calm hot ocean, with the sandy sea side and the hot sun's reflection from the sand, was heard by the whales and smelt by my grandmother, it was tasted by the fish and touched by me, I found myself in Dubai.

_____

_____

_____

_____

Fun for all the family! This is certainly my experience of CentreParks.

_____

Spain meant for him that there was no school, no homework, but also no stress. Just living his life to the best when he was there!

_____

_____

Sunbathing on the beach, the sound of the birds circling above the sea and the splash of the waves on the shoreline.

_____

_____

Activity 2

1 Make a vocabulary word bank to describe a trip to see this volcano.

2 Now look at the following exam question:

Write a letter to your friend explaining why you would like him or her to join you on a trip to Stromboli, an island near Italy, to visit the volcano. **(16 marks)**

Write the first **two** paragraphs in response to this question, using vocabulary from the word bank you have made.

Continue ▶

_____
_____
_____
_____
_____
_____
_____
_____

3 Check your work against the success criteria below. Have you:
- proofread for sentence sense, paragraphing, punctuation and spelling
- used a variety of sentence structures
- used a variety of punctuation
- used a variety of engaging vocabulary?

4 Complete your response below, remembering to check against the success criteria.

_____
_____
_____
_____
_____
_____
_____
_____
_____
_____
_____
_____

Continue ▶

Continue ▸

Activity 3

20 minutes

1 Read the examination question below.

> **Write a letter of complaint from a package holiday tourist to his travel company for the disorganised reaction to the chaos caused by a volcanic eruption and the impact on his travel plans. Outline the problems encountered and suggest how the travel company should compensate for them.** **(16 marks)**

2 You are now going to proofread the opening section of a student's response to this question. Annotate the extract with any corrections you would suggest. Write out a best version of any sentences that need reworking in the space above the relevant sentence.

Dear Sirs, I am writing to you as a result of your disasterous

reaction to the Icelandic volcano chaos of last week and

to ask for compensation for the extensive expenses that I

incured as a result of the travel companys incompetance.

While I am one of the lucky ones that is now ablto continue

with my work and has now managed to return home, this was

purely a result of my own actions rather than any activity

by your travel company. As a result, I have had to incur the

costs of my personal secretary and the significant expense

of a rail ticket from Spain to France and then an additional

train ticket on the Eurostar. I would have expected more care

and attention from your travel company since myself and my

family had booked a relatively costly luxury package that you

yourself said would be 'tailored to my needs'. This was hardly

the case in this instance, I have enclosed the receipts for my

expenses which I will expect you to meet in full.

Activity 4

10 minutes

Proofread your complete response for Activity 2 starting on page 69. List any suggestions for alterations that you would make as a result of what you have learnt from the proofreading exercise in Activity 3.

Suggestions for improvement:

_____

_____

_____

_____

_____

Re-read the exam question and student answer in Activity 3, pages 74–75.

Use the table below to check that you have identified and corrected examples of **each** of these points for improvement.

	Tick or cross
Spelling corrections of complex words	
Paragraphing	
Varied punctuation	
Varied sentence structures	
Short sentences for effect	
Punctuation for effect	

Read the following examiner comment about the student answer. Then complete the Tips and practice section opposite.

Examiner comment

There is a range of formal vocabulary here and the register is maintained appropriately. There are several examples of spelling errors of more complex words. Paragraphing has not been addressed, which affects the overall grade of this piece. Punctuation and sentence structures are not varied in this student's work, with heavy reliance on complex sentences and full stops. The student needs to demonstrate a more conscious use of short sentences and punctuation for effect.

Tips and practice

Tips

Write down or discuss what you have learnt about:

Proofreading sentences: _____

_____

Proofreading punctuation: _____

_____

Proofreading sentences and vocabulary: _____

_____

Practice

Now apply what you have learnt to all your writing practice:

1 Set time aside to proofread in the exam.
2 Ensure that you vary punctuation and vocabulary in your writing answers.
3 Check that all sentences are secure.

RAISE MY GRADE

Skills to raise my grade

Now that you have completed this lesson on proofreading, fill in the RAG table below to see if your confidence has improved.

	R	A	G
I can recognise when sentences are secure or insecure.	◯	◯	◯
I can use a range of punctuation accurately.	◯	◯	◯
I can use a range of vocabulary that is accurately spelt.	◯	◯	◯
I always proofread my written work.	◯	◯	◯

You will answer **two** Writing questions in the AQA GCSE English and English Language exam.

In order to 'communicate effectively' you need to identify exactly **who** you are writing for, what **form** the writing should take and what **features** of writing you need to demonstrate. You can use the TAP technique (text type, audience, purpose) that you are already familiar with from your Reading work before planning a Writing answer.

Think carefully about the kind of language you should use in relation to the topic and also whether you should write informally or formally (the register). Beware of writing very informally. Even if the exam question encourages you to write informally you need to display a range of interesting vocabulary and your command of the English language! You must ensure that your vocabulary and style show flair and interest the reader.

This lesson will support you in pinpointing exactly what a question is asking you to do and identifying the features you need to show to gain the best marks possible.

Skills to raise my grade

Fill in the RAG table below to show how confident you are in the following areas:	R	A	G
I can identify the text type, audience and purpose required of a Writing exam question.	◯	◯	◯
I can write in a variety of forms and demonstrate their appropriate presentational, structural and language features.	◯	◯	◯
I can identify an appropriate register (when to write formally and when to write informally).	◯	◯	◯

Activity 1

10 minutes

Choose **three** of the text types below and list the features you would expect to find in them.

informal letter	formal letter	
report	leaflet	newspaper article
speech	review	magazine article

Text 1: _Report_

Features: _heading, sub-heading(s), author name, bullet points, (image), (caption),_

date, paragraph

Register: _____

Text 2: _____

Features: _____

_____

Register: _____

Text 3: _____

Features: _____

_____

Register: _____

Text 4: _____

Features: _____

_____

Register: _____

Activity 2

15 minutes

1 Identify the TAP, register and structural features of the following exam question.

> **Write a front page newspaper article for the local newspaper, the *Witney Gazette*, about a charity fire walking event.**
>
> **(24 marks)**

T: _____

A: _____

P: _____

Register (formal/informal) = _____

Presentational and structural features = _____

_____

_____

2 In order to write your newspaper article, read the following transcript of a video about the fire walking event, underlining anything that you think might be useful to include in your writing.

The Fire Walkers of Witney

11 March 2010 … A group of brave individuals take off their shoes and socks and walk on a 20ft-long bed of burning wood for charity.

37 volunteers removed their shoes and socks for a charity fire walk in Witney town square…

Participant 1: I'm really looking forward to it. We're all pretty charged up so it should be good.

Interviewer: How charged up?

Participant 1: I dunno, pretty charged up. We all pretty charged up? Yeah, pretty good.

Interviewer: What attracted you to do fire walking?

Participant 2: I have no idea. It was his fault.

Interviewer: Why do you want to do it?

Vicar 1: Well, I just want to raise a lot of money for a good cause, really. I mean Helen and Douglas House is a really really worthwhile charity and we should just give as much as we can to them.

Vicar 2: Well we're gonna do this fire walk and I'm gonna do it because Toby told me I had to do it. He came to us and he said we're gonna … three clergyman who are trustees of base 33, have to do this fire walk. He didn't give me any choice. He didn't ask me, he just said you're gonna do it.

Interviewer: What about you, sir?

Vicar 3: Well I'm doing it for base 33, for the young people. So, I think that's it really … I wouldn't do it otherwise. It's absolute insanity, madness.

Interviewer: Does this fire walk have an ecclesiastical sort of ring to it?

Vicar 4: Well, ur, there are people who said to me that it's a bit pagan, but actually if we look into the Old Testament we see Shadrach, Meshach and Abednego go wandering in that and apparently some monks in islands off Greece have been doing this as a spiritual discipline in order to bring them nearer to God as well, so I don't think there's a problem there.

Interviewer: You're not going down that route, you're just gonna do it for a good cause.

Participant 3: Just doing it for a good cause, good night out and I hope lots of fun.

Participant 4: I've always been interested in this and um I just thought, well, now's the moment. You know, I'm getting on a bit, now's my chance.

Interviewer: How many times have you walked on the fire?

Organiser 1: [laughter] err, we take it in turns so probably about 500 times. At least.

Interviewer: And you've never burned your feet?

Organiser 1: No. I wouldn't do it again if I had.

Organiser 2: We've been doing this for 26 years now. We have no injuries, no accidents, no incidents of any kind. What we like to do is come along, do our fire walking, and leave people behind with happy faces and mucky feet. That's what we like and lots of money raised for the causes close to their heart.

Participant 5: It's gonna be really good. We're gonna have a really good session with um Karen here um who will get us all in the frame of mind where we're actually able to take that first step to walk the 20 feet along the fire track.

[band plays and fire walk is prepared]
[claps and cheers]

MC: Listen, guys. First of all I'd like to say please do not try this at home for obvious reasons. These guys have been trained up to do this for the last 2 hours. All I'm asking for you is if you could give each and every one of them the biggest Jerry Springer round of applause. Thank you very much!

[claps and cheers as each participant fire walks]

Participant 3: That's been a fantastic evening, absolutely wonderful. Such fun, and just amazing that everyone went through with it, and 100% success and … absolutely tremendous and wonderful to watch the confidence of people as they got ready for it and prepared for it, went outside, saw the fire and then got going and walked across it. Absolutely tremendous.

Activity 3

30 minutes

Complete your article in answer to the question in Activity 2, page 80, as follows:

Write a front page newspaper article for the local newspaper, the *Witney Gazette*, about a charity fire walking event.

(24 marks)

Continue ▸

Continue ▸

Activity 4

10 minutes

Read the excerpt from a B grade answer below, along with the A grade criteria.
What improvements can be made to the answer so that it fulfils the A grade criteria?

List your improvements for the student below:

 grade answer

Witney Gazette
WITNEY VICARS WALK ON WATER

Jesus might have walked on water to gain points with his audience, but local vicars are now walking on fire to impress their congregations.

They were joined by lots of other people in their unusual pastime. Accompanied by the notes of the Witney brass band. no one burnt their feet and £2500 was raised for charity. The spectacle was great. A range of local people turned out to support the event despite the weather. 'A good cause, a good night out and I hope lots of fun' was how one local described the event.

> picture of vicar walking across the fire walk

A
▶ Engages the local reader with vivid detail, facts and local references
▶ Writes a formal newspaper article using a variety of sophisticated vocabulary and sentence structures
▶ Employs a variety of paragraphs and sentence structures appropriate for a local newspaper
▶ Uses a variety of linguistic devices and vocabulary to inform and entertain
▶ Establishes and maintains a journalistic angle on the story, for example, local charity fundraising, 'eccentric Witney'

Tip 1: _____

_____

Tip 2: _____

_____

Tip 3: _____

_____

Here are extracts from two student responses to the following exam question:

> Write a tabloid newspaper front page story to go out on 1st April.
> In the tradition of past April Fool stories, the form and language will need to convince the readers of the truth of the April Fool's joke.
>
> (16 marks)

Read the answers together with the examiner comments, before completing the Tips and practice section opposite.

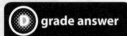 **grade answer**

Student A

> The Education Minster announced today that schools will now be run by MI5, the Uk's Securite Service. Hot on the heels of his rule that teachers will now be recruited from the army, Mi5 have Said they think their the best people to do the job. The head of MI5 said We will be able to get the best grades possible for pupils. We can also quickly spot pupils who are not fitting in to expectations of behavour and attendance. We are the ones to deal with them.

Examiner comment

The candidate engages the reader with an amusing storyline. The response includes factual details and uses direct speech appropriately. However, shorter sentences and paragraphs are needed for a tabloid newspaper and there are errors in spelling and punctuation.

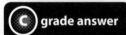 **grade answer**

Student B

> The education Minister announced today that all students will be given porridge before starting lessons in school. This will be a compulsory part of the school day and will give everyone a good start.
> "It's been good enough for me for years and has got me where I am today. Porridge is a nutritous and wholesome food. Too many children today are going to school without a good breakfast and this is one reason for underachevement,' he told teachers at Wildon High school, during a visit this morning.
> Jamie Oliver, celebrity chef, has supported this move. He has suggested he will be publishing a booklet for schools of exciting new porridge recipes for today's students.

Examiner comment

This candidate creates an engaging story to interest readers and includes appropriate factual information. The response uses the short paragraphs and simple sentence structures appropriate for a tabloid format. A range of interesting vocabulary is included and there is generally accurate spelling and punctuation.

Tips and practice

Tips

Write down or discuss what you have learnt about:

TAPping your question: _____

_____

Writing in a particular form: _____

_____

Practice

Now apply what you have learnt to all your writing practice.

1 TAP your exam question.
2 Demonstrate the features that the writing form requires.
3 Demonstrate a formal or informal style, as required by the question, through your
   sentence structures, punctuation and vocabulary.

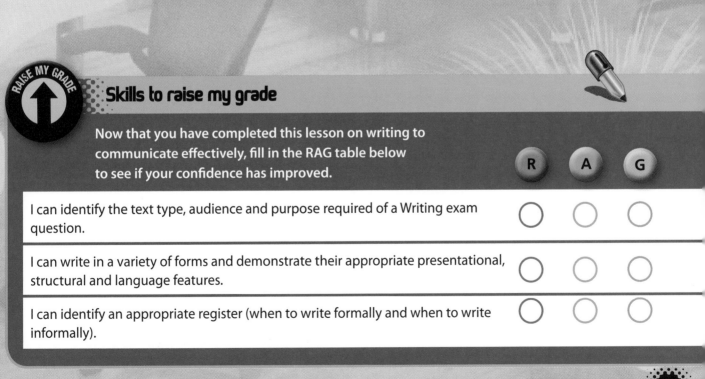

Skills to raise my grade

Now that you have completed this lesson on writing to communicate effectively, fill in the RAG table below to see if your confidence has improved.

	R	A	G
I can identify the text type, audience and purpose required of a Writing exam question.	○	○	○
I can write in a variety of forms and demonstrate their appropriate presentational, structural and language features.	○	○	○
I can identify an appropriate register (when to write formally and when to write informally).	○	○	○

By working through these revision lessons you have now revisited the AQA GCSE English skills you learnt during your English lessons. Part of your success in the exam lies in your knowledge of these English skills. Another part lies in your application of these skills, together with your exam technique. Now it is time to apply your skills to the exam papers.

Throughout the revision lessons you have addressed English skills and collected exam tips from both the materials and your teacher. This section brings everything together. Part 1 checks on your exam technique. You will then apply your English skills to some exam-style questions in part 2.

Part 1: exam technique

Look at the exam questions that follow on pages 88–95. Using what you've learnt and revised, plan how you would tackle each question in an exam situation.

Do not answer the exam questions themselves but use the boxes provided to make notes, highlight key words and phrases and generally plan your answer. You will write your actual answer in Part 2 of this section.

> What do you need to identify about this article before you begin work on it?

Read **Item 1 'Review: Caroline Cardus sees How to Look Good Naked ... with a Difference'**, and answer the question below.

> Identify the key words in the question

1 What, according to the article, do you learn about Caroline Cardus and her viewpoint about Gok Wan's programme?

> Which sections of the source text will you underline?

> Will you use quotations in your answer?

Item 1

You are here: **Home > Features > Reviews >** How to Look Good Naked

Review: Caroline Cardus sees How to Look Good Naked... with a Difference

5 February 2010

By Caroline Cardus

For the last three weeks I've been watching Gok Wan's somewhat awkwardly titled 'How To Look Good Naked... With a Difference'.

I was dearly hoping the 'difference' would be that the programme didn't include the more common gaffes some disability programmes make. Late last year, an email from the production company asking for disabled women to take part appeared in my inbox, but I chose not to go for it to avoid being caught up in said gaffes. Pleasingly, on the whole they didn't materialise.

This overall lack of gaffes was a disappointment to friends on Facebook who'd challenged me to a drinking game - one shot downed for every time Gok said 'brave'. (There were a couple of occasions when he did - although it was in a shopping centre full of screaming women when somebody was about to go starkers. So I was prepared to be ambiguous about the use of the word).

Despite my cynicism about HTLGN... With a Difference, Gok won my respect. He's one of those people who is prepared to say 'I haven't done this before and I don't know how we're going to do it - but let's try, because it needs to be addressed'. He's a force of nature who disarms and charms you with his ebullient manner and genuine people skills.

He clearly respects his 'girlfriends', although refreshingly, he isn't afraid to challenge and criticise deftly within his own specialism. Herein lies the way forward to comfortable inclusion: respect, confidence in your own expertise, willingness to listen and good ol' openness and honesty. If more presenters working with disabled people had these skills then this emerging area would have an easier ride.

These three episodes packed a lot in. I understand there is much to do in fashion when it comes to accepting and representing difference regarding impairment, representation and body shape. But I also felt they would have benefited from dealing with less content in more depth.

Whilst I looked forward to comprehensive fashion advice, as the content whirled through the makeover, the campaign, the Q and A sessions, the photo session and finally, the naked unveiling, I found few tips that I hadn't already sussed out and was left wanting more.

Issues are unfortunately part of everyday life for disabled people. Perhaps the disabled Cinderellas who like fluffy fashion telly might well be crying, "thank you for the acknowledgement, but can we have more frocks and shoes please?" The issue is that we want to know how to look good with our clothes on!

But these programmes are also a journey. Gok's approach is that the dichotomy between confidence and fashion must be explored before his girl emerges as a princess. Add the disability 'issue' into the mix and it's not surprising things got a little complicated. Luckily because the programme did make relatively few gaffes I was sober enough to take it all in.

It's worth noting that some inspired moments came out of it too. In episode three, Gok presents Di Cram with a tactile and audio 'style book' to help her picture what shape of clothes suit her best. I'm willing to bet there were visually impaired people up and down the country wishing they could get their mitts on something like that too.

There were interesting statistics included throughout the programmes to underline the disability focus. They gave statistics on how many disabled consumers there are - and how many felt disability was not represented on the High Street.

I also felt the images that came out of Nikki Fox and Natasha Wood's ad campaign would work well in the mainstream and promoted fashion and inclusion in a way the general public could digest. There's still the whole 'acceptably pretty slim girl sitting in a wheelchair' fashion issue, but lets not pretend shows like this are meant for the serious emancipated feminist.

In conclusion, I hope the initiative shown doesn't stop here with the production company ticking the equality box and never hereafter having a disabled person on the show.

Ideally, the next step would be to regularly see disabled people integrated into 'Look Good Naked', and for it to focus on disability fashion themes again in the future. Looking around the internet during the last three weeks has shown me the programmes were well received and even went beyond expectations, so it would be a step backwards if nothing more happens.

Now use the space below to plan your answer to question 1.

(8 marks)

How long should you spend on this question?

Approximately how many separate points will you make in answer to this question?

Now read **Item 2 'Jorvik Viking Centre'**, and answer the question below.

2 Explain how the presentation and layout add to the effectiveness of the text.

> Will you use quotations in your answer?

> Identify the key words in the question

Item 2

THE JOURNEY THROUGH JORVIK

Smells Key
- 01 Fish Smells
- 02 Farmyard Smells
- 03 Burning Logs
- 04 Molten Iron
- 05 Roasting Boar
- 06 Smells of the Market

Map Key
- A Activity
- Gallery
- ★ Meet a Viking
- Meet an Archaeologist
- Men's Toilets
- Women's Toilets
- Disabled Toilets
- **F** Fire Exit

GET FACE TO FACE WITH THE VIKINGS AS YOU DELVE FURTHER INTO YORK'S VIKING PAST.

Are you a Viking?
Using this unique exhibition you can discover how the Vikings have influenced your life and see if you could in fact be a Viking!

Artefacts Alive
Our four holographic Viking ghosts will introduce you to 800 Viking-age finds and explain how some of these items were used in every day life.

Unearthed
Stories of Viking-age life, death, battle and disease can all be revealed through the examination of 10th -11th century bones. See a skeleton of a Viking killed in battle and discover what secrets he can tell.

Now use the space below to plan your answer to question 2.

(8 marks)

How long should you spend on this question?

Approximately how many separate points will you make in answer to this question?

List the features of the advert you will comment on in relation to the question

Now read **Item 3 'Over the top into Lancashire'**, which is a chapter from a non-fiction book. The writer, Simon Armitage, conveys his experiences of the north of England where he was born and still lives. Answer the question that follows.

Identify the key words in the question

3 What are Armitage's thoughts and feelings about seeing one of his old clients?

Will you use quotations in your answer?

Item 3

Over the Top into Lancashire

Helping somebody move house, driving a lorry through Lees, you pull up as a kid steps out on to a pedestrian crossing. You can't remember his name but you know his face. You were the duty officer at Oldham Magistrates when he was sentenced. As a juvenile, he stood silently in front of the witness box with his mother at his side, waiting for the decision. The chief magistrate that day was a dark-haired woman in her fifties. A few months before, you'd been sitting behind her at a liaison meeting as someone from Probation tried to explain the benefits of Community Service. She leaned across to one of her colleagues and whispered in a loud voice, 'Me, I just send them all to prison'.

The boy waited, staring at the ceiling, as the magistrates filed back into court from the retiring-room and took their places on the bench. She'd only just got the words 'custodial-sentence' out of her mouth when he leaned forward, extended his arm towards her, offered the thin, white patch of his wrist, then dragged a razor blade across it with his hand.

Sprung from its normal circuit, blood is a wild and lively substance, and carries within it one last effort of will, like the leap of a man from a burning house. There was a moment of suspension, like in a painting, a Chagall, with bodies hanging in mid-air; the fat policeman dropping down from above; the magistrate diving sideways for the door with a thick, oily scream flowing from her mouth; the boy with his hand still raised, his long crimson arm reaching out towards her with its fingertips on fire.

You watch him stride from one side of the road to the other with his hands in his pockets, as the green man on the pedestrian crossing flashes on and off then turns to red. The lights change and you move off.

Now use the space below to plan your answer to question 3.

(8 marks)

How long should you spend on this question?

Approximately how many separate points will you make in answer to this question?

4 Now look at **Item 3** and **either** of the other items on pages 89–91. Compare the way in which language is used in both texts to convey the writer's viewpoint. Give some examples and comment on their effect on the reader.

Which item will you choose and why?

Which are the key words in the question you will underline?

(16 marks)

Part 2: applying English skills to exam questions

You are now going to build on this preparation and the work you have completed in exam technique by writing full, exam-style answers in timed conditions.

Section A: Reading

Answer **all** questions

You are advised to spend about one hour on this section.

Read **Item 1 'Review: Caroline Cardus sees How to Look Good Naked … with a Difference'**, and answer the question below.

1 What, according to the article, do you learn about Caroline Cardus and her viewpoint about Gok Wan's programme?

Item 1

You are here: **Home** > **Features** > **Reviews** > How to Look Good Naked

Review: Caroline Cardus sees How to Look Good Naked... with a Difference

5 February 2010

By Caroline Cardus

For the last three weeks I've been watching Gok Wan's somewhat awkwardly titled 'How To Look Good Naked... With a Difference'.

I was dearly hoping the 'difference' would be that the programme didn't include the more common gaffes some disability programmes make. Late last year, an email from the production company asking for disabled women to take part appeared in my inbox, but I chose not to go for it to avoid being caught up in said gaffes. Pleasingly, on the whole they didn't materialise.

This overall lack of gaffes was a disappointment to friends on Facebook who'd challenged me to a drinking game - one shot downed for every time Gok said 'brave'. (There were a couple of occasions when he did - although it was in a shopping centre full of screaming women when somebody was about to go starkers. So I was prepared to be ambiguous about the use of the word).

Despite my cynicism about HTLGN... With a Difference, Gok won my respect. He's one of those people who is prepared to say 'I haven't done this before and I don't know how we're going to do it - but let's try, because it needs to be addressed'. He's a force of nature who disarms and charms you with his ebullient manner and genuine people skills.

He clearly respects his 'girlfriends', although refreshingly, he isn't afraid to challenge and criticise deftly within his own specialism. Herein lies the way forward to comfortable inclusion: respect, confidence in your own expertise, willingness to listen and good ol' openness and honesty. If more presenters working with disabled people had these skills then this emerging area would have an easier ride.

These three episodes packed a lot in. I understand there is much to do in fashion when it comes to accepting and representing difference regarding impairment, representation and body shape. But I also felt they would have benefited from dealing with less content in more depth.

Whilst I looked forward to comprehensive fashion advice, as the content whirled through the makeover, the campaign, the Q and A sessions, the photo session and finally, the naked unveiling, I found few tips that I hadn't already sussed out and was left wanting more.

Issues are unfortunately part of everyday life for disabled people. Perhaps the disabled Cinderellas who like fluffy fashion telly might well be crying, "thank you for the acknowledgement, but can we have more frocks and shoes please?" The issue is that we want to know how to look good with our clothes on!

But these programmes are also a journey. Gok's approach is that the dichotomy between confidence and fashion must be explored before his girl emerges as a princess. Add the disability 'issue' into the mix and it's not surprising things got a little complicated. Luckily because the programme did make relatively few gaffes I was sober enough to take it all in.

It's worth noting that some inspired moments came out of it too. In episode three, Gok presents Di Cram with a tactile and audio 'style book' to help her picture what shape of clothes suit her best. I'm willing to bet there were visually impaired people up and down the country wishing they could get their mitts on something like that too.

There were interesting statistics included throughout the programmes to underline the disability focus. They gave statistics on how many disabled consumers there are - and how many felt disability was not represented on the High Street.

I also felt the images that came out of Nikki Fox and Natasha Wood's ad campaign would work well in the mainstream and promoted fashion and inclusion in a way the general public could digest. There's still the whole 'acceptably pretty slim girl sitting in a wheelchair' fashion issue, but lets not pretend shows like this are meant for the serious emancipated feminist.

In conclusion, I hope the initiative shown doesn't stop here with the production company ticking the equality box and never hereafter having a disabled person on the show.

Ideally, the next step would be to regularly see disabled people integrated into 'Look Good Naked', and for it to focus on disability fashion themes again in the future. Looking around the internet during the last three weeks has shown me the programmes were well received and even went beyond expectations, so it would be a step backwards if nothing more happens.

(8 marks)

Now read **Item 2 'Jorvik Viking Centre'**, and answer the question below.

2 Explain how the presentation and layout add to the effectiveness of the text.

Item 2

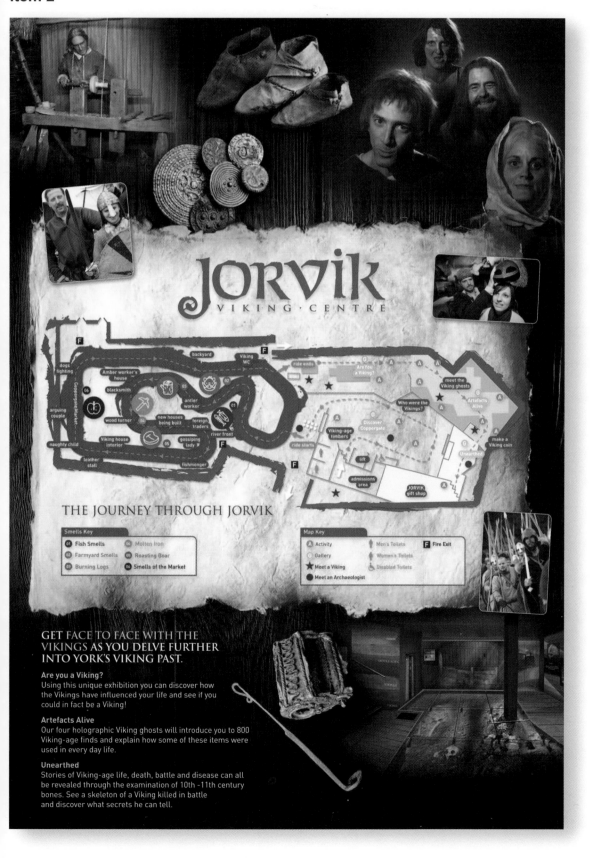

(8 marks)

Now read **Item 3**, a chapter from a non-fiction book, by the writer, Simon Armitage, and answer the question below.

3 Comment on Armitage's thoughts and feelings about seeing one of his old clients.

Item 3

Over the Top into Lancashire

Helping somebody move house, driving a lorry through Lees, you pull up as a kid steps out on to a pedestrian crossing. You can't remember his name but you know his face. You were the duty officer at Oldham Magistrates when he was sentenced. As a juvenile, he stood silently in front of the witness box with his mother at his side, waiting for the decision. The chief magistrate that day was a dark-haired woman in her fifties. A few months before, you'd been sitting behind her at a liaison meeting as someone from Probation tried to explain the benefits of Community Service. She leaned across to one of her colleagues and whispered in a loud voice, 'Me, I just send them all to prison'.

The boy waited, staring at the ceiling, as the magistrates filed back into court from the retiring-room and took their places on the bench. She'd only just got the words 'custodial-sentence' out of her mouth when he leaned forward, extended his arm towards her, offered the thin, white patch of his wrist, then dragged a razor blade across it with his hand.

Sprung from its normal circuit, blood is a wild and lively substance, and carries within it one last effort of will, like the leap of a man from a burning house. There was a moment of suspension, like in a painting, a Chagall, with bodies hanging in mid-air; the fat policeman dropping down from above; the magistrate diving sideways for the door with a thick, oily scream flowing from her mouth; the boy with his hand still raised, his long crimson arm reaching out towards her with its fingertips on fire.

You watch him stride from one side of the road to the other with his hands in his pockets, as the green man on the pedestrian crossing flashes on and off then turns to red. The lights change and you move off.

(8 marks)

Now look at **all three** items.

4 Look at Item 3 and either of the other items. Compare the way in which language is used in both texts to convey the writer's viewpoint. Give some examples and comment on their effect on the reader.

_____

_____

_____

_____

_____

_____

_____

_____

_____

_____

_____

_____

_____

_____

_____

_____

_____

_____

_____

_____

_____

_____

_____

(16 marks)

Section B: Writing

Answer **both** questions in this section.

You are advised to spend about one hour on this section.

---

1 You are the parent of a new student to a school who will be in a wheelchair throughout his secondary school career. Write a letter to the headteacher to outline your child's particular needs and how you believe they should be met at the school.

_____

_____

_____

_____

_____

_____

_____

_____

_____

_____

_____

_____

_____

_____

_____

_____

_____

(16 marks)

2 Write a descriptive piece that conveys a strong sense of a place that you know well.

_____

_____

_____

_____

_____

_____

_____

_____

_____

_____

_____

_____

_____

_____

_____

_____

_____

_____

_____

_____

_____

_____

_____

_____

_____

_____

(24 marks)